ANGEL NUMBERS MASTERY

ANGEL NUMBERS MASTERY

EVERYTHING YOU NEED TO KNOW ABOUT ANGEL NUMBERS AND WHAT THEY MEAN FOR YOU

Sarahdawn Tunis

P.O. Box 150846
Lakewood, CO 80215
Sarahdawntunis.com

Copyright © 2018 Sarahdawn Tunis

All rights reserved. No part of this book may be reproduced by any mechanical, photographic or electronic process, or in the form of audio recording, nor may it be stored in a retrieval system, transmitted, or otherwise be copied for public or private use – other than for "fair use" as brief quotations embodied in articles and reviews - without the written permission of the publisher.

The author of this book does not dispense medical or psychological advice or prescribe the use of any technique as a form of treatment for physical, emotional, or medical problems without the advice of a physician, either directly or indirectly. The intent of the author is only to provide general information to assist you along your path to emotional and spiritual well-being. In the event you use any of the information in this book for yourself, the author and the publisher assume no responsibility for your actions.

Published in the United States of America by:
Sarahdawn Tunis
P.O. Box 150846
Lakewood, Colorado 80215
www.sarahdawntunis.com

ISBN: 978-1-7315-9680-2

DEDICATION

This book is respectfully dedicated to all those who believed in me when I had yet learned to believe in myself. It is because of you I have the faith, love and determination to write this book from my heart and soul and pass on the gift you have given me to others.

Acknowledgements

I'd like to send out the biggest, warmest and heartfelt thank you to my three wonderful boys. To Nathanial, my biggest supporter, thank you for taking care of your brothers on so many days so I could work on this book. All the nights you made dinner, entertained your little brothers and encouraged me to continue even in my times of doubt. I don't know where I would be without you and I certainly would have never finished this book without your help. To Nicholas and Dominic, thank you for your sacrifice and understanding as I spent all those long days and nights on the computer. And especially for those times when you had to wait for me to "finish this part" before making dinner. I love you guys so very much.

A special thank you to Archangel Raphael who assisted my health even when my doctors wouldn't. For helping me through all those days of feeling tired and sick and overall helping me feel well enough to keep working every day until this book was complete.

To my guardian angels and all the angels who gave me the inspiration and words to write this book. Thank you for angel numbers and your love, guidance and support. Thank you for all the years you helped me work through my depression and gave me the courage and confidence to continue after the traumatic loss of my husband. Who knows where I would be if you hadn't whispered in my ear that day.

I also want to thank Sarah Balog, of Cape and Tiara, Inc, who found me through my blog one day and turned into my biggest motivator, both for writing this book and for life in general. Thank you for all the long emails, all the encouragement to keep going, and the donations you sent - especially the one you sent for pizza night when I wasn't feeling well. You are an amazing person and I love you so very much.

To Melissa Brunoehler, my beta reader. Thank you for your help, support and the useful comments and suggestions you gave me for making this book better than I could have done on my own. Thank you for taking the time to read through my book a few times even while you were busy starting up your coaching business. If you want a wonderful life coach, check out Melissa at Its Your Life Coaching.

To my mother, Nancy, who put a roof over my head and made sure the boys and I always had a warm home with lots of internet service. Providing me the opportunity to work on my dream of writing. Without you, I never could have written this book especially while I homeschooled my boys.

To Sara Harris, my Godmother, for all the love and support she has always given throughout the years. Beginning when I was little, she has given me the confidence and love and support to encourage and enable me to write this book and follow my dreams. Thank you.

CONTENTS

Acknowledgments	vi
Introduction	xi

PART ONE: ANGEL NUMBER MESSAGES

Chapter 1	Introduction to Angel Numbers	1
Chapter 2	Why Angels Use Numbers	6
Chapter 3	Where Angel Numbers Come From	11
Chapter 4	Which Numbers Are Angel Numbers	15
Chapter 5	Types of Angel Numbers	20
Chapter 6	Sequences and Number Combinations	28
Chapter 7	Receiving Angel Number Messages	41
Chapter 8	Understanding Your Messages	49
Chapter 9	Your Angel Numbers	67
Chapter 10	When Angel Numbers Stop	74
Chapter 11	Increasing Your Awareness	82

PART TWO: GUIDE TO ANGEL NUMBERS

How to Use This Guide		101
Angel Number 1	*"New Beginnings"*	104
Angel Number 2	*"Keep the Faith"*	109
Angel Number 3	*"On the Right Path"*	115
Angel Number 4	*"Time to Focus"*	121
Angel Number 5	*"On Wings of Change"*	126
Angel Number 6	*"Too Much Worry"*	132
Angel Number 7	*"Keep It Up"*	138
Angel Number 8	*"Infinite Potential"*	144
Angel Number 9	*"Your Soul's Mission"*	150
Angel Number 0	*"God's Loving Embrace"*	157
Angel Number 11	*"The Doorway"*	163
Angel Number 22	*"Dream Maker"*	169
Angel Number 33	*"Pass It On"*	176
Conclusion		184
About The Author		187
Source Notes		188

INTRODUCTION

Angel numbers have been a significant part of my life for several years now. I find them to be a constant companion, always there, always reliable and always pushing me to be the best person I can be.

But I haven't always taken the easiest path in life; either because of the choices I've made, or just where life has taken me. Beginning in my teens, I became consumed by depression, anxiety and thinking the world was better off without me. Not believing in myself and being depressed took me down a very difficult path. I've struggled with abuse, financial problems, being a widow and single parent, and feeling lost, alone and unloved. All of it creating feelings of worthlessness, doubt and fear.

It wasn't until I was facing the loss of everything that I let go of the need to please everyone else and I found my true-self through the loving encouragement of the angels. I sort of stumbled upon the angels, but once I did, my life changed. I discovered a love for myself that I had never experienced before. This love came from God and was amplified through the angels. It radiated throughout my very being.

When I first heard about angel numbers, I thought they were

interesting, but I didn't see them as anything exceptional. In fact, I was aware of angel numbers for quite some time before I began to learn the value they would eventually have on the rest of my life. It happened when going through another intense relapse of depression. Feeling overwhelmed and consumed by wanting my life to just be over. I felt distant and blocked from the angels I had previously come to know. My inner-voice telling me that I was so worthless God and even the angels were somehow disappointed in me.

Out of shame, I resisted the angels, their love and their help. Yet despite these feelings of shame, despair and worthlessness, I began noticing repeating numbers all around me. Numbers and patterns of numbers that were odd or out of the ordinary appeared along my path consistently. It seemed as if someone was intentionally placing these numbers in front of me. Although I shrugged them off at first, the persistence of these numbers eventually began to give me hope and a sense of empowerment. Leading me down a path of healing.

I continued to see the numbers even after I began to feel better. And soon after decided I really wanted to understand what angel numbers are and what they mean for me. After getting back on track and spending several months studying and researching angel numbers, I felt guided to stop taking anti-depressants and take control of my life. Now, several years later, I have not looked back. Angel numbers have served to help me be successful, find my own worth and talents and see life from an entirely different perspective. Looking back on the old depressed me is now like watching a sad movie. As if I have grown into an entirely different person. No longer in touch with the depression that used to consume me so entirely.

Although the angels have assisted me along my journey in many ways, it is the angel numbers that have kept me on my path through the toughest of times. Serving as a constant reminder that

Introduction

I am loved, never forgotten and destined to follow my life path. As you will see in the stories I include throughout this book, angel numbers are what have, and continue, to get me over the biggest of obstacles and challenges.

That is not to say I don't have hard days or never experience doubt. That is what I love the most about angel numbers. Even when I experience the human emotions and thoughts that take me away from my angels and from my life purpose, the numbers still come through. Bringing me back to my spiritual nature and propelling me forward in faith. Faith in both the spiritual and in myself.

So this book is meant to share with you what I have learned and what the angels have taught me along the way about angel numbers, how to use them and how to understand what the messages mean. I have tried to include as much helpful information as possible so that you, too, can understand the power these signs have in your life.

This book is in two parts. Part one goes over what angel numbers are and why they are so important in our lives. It goes into further detail about how to receive and understand angel number messages. Part two is a guide for the primary angel numbers, which includes the major keywords, the energy and several possible messages that the number may have.

I have created this book as a way for you to master angel numbers and use them with ease throughout your day to day life. Through the good times, bad times, confusing times and times when you're faced with a decision you are uncertain about – it is my hope this book will help you use and understand angel numbers to get you through it all a bit easier than going at it alone.

The guide and some of the concepts in this book are also included in my blog at sarahdawntunis.com/angel-numbers. This book contains much more detail and is aimed at helping you understand angel numbers on a deeper level, but I do keep the blog updated with more numbers and combinations of numbers. So, feel free to check it out and use it in addition to this book.

In both this book and my blog, the information about the energy of each number is based on numerology. Numerology is the study of the energy of numbers and goes back to ancient times. Much of what you will read corresponds with numerology and is based on what we know about each number. I have put this information together in an easy to read and understand format.

However, I do not write alone, I write with the angels. Prior to each writing session, I do a meditation and ask the angels for assistance in passing on the information they want people to know. Many of the messages and information you get from my blog and this book I have channeled. Meaning it comes from the angels assisting me. This information is meant to enhance and pass on more meaning to you as the reader. So, you will find some of the information and messages are unique to my blog and this book.

I wish you the best and truly hope this book assists you in tapping into the power angel numbers can have along your path and in your day to day life.

With love, light and blessings,

Sarahdawn

PART ONE
ANGEL NUMBER MESSAGES

CHAPTER ONE
INTRODUCTION TO ANGEL NUMBERS

Life isn't always what it seems. Beneath the existence of the world we know, is a foundation lying completely out of awareness. A foundation that goes unnoticed and unseen as we live our daily lives. As human beings, we are restricted by space, time and the five senses. Our physical bodies limiting us and binding us to the physical world. It is easy to become tethered to the notion that reality is simply, what you see is what you get. Especially since that is what we are commonly taught to believe. And on the surface, it makes sense.

Yet, if you have picked up this book and began to read the pages within, you are probably aware that there is much more to reality. More than what many physical beings believe. You feel there is something more. Aware of forces beyond what you can see, hear, smell, taste and touch. Something that guides your existence in this life to more. More than just being. More than just surviving. You are not just a physical being, you are also a spiritual one.

There is a strong connection between our physical world and the spiritual world. Both worlds overlapping. The spiritual, surrounding, intertwined and interacting with our physical world. Many people never notice it and some even chose to ignore it, but either way, the spiritual world is there and available for us to tap into. It provides a way to ease our isolation and misery in this lifetime, find our purpose and even make the planet a better place for everyone.

The easiest way for us to access the spiritual world is through energy. The world and all things in it are made up of energy. Our very beings and everything we are exposed to are comprised of this energy. Interestingly, in the basic construction of that energy, you will find numbers. Each number resonating at a different frequency and carrying specific and unique vibrations. The vibrations of each number bouncing off and integrating with each other in a harmonious and synchronized dance. A beautiful and masterful creation of reality.

Even if you are like me and not mathematically inclined, knowing about the energy of numbers and how they influence us in the physical world is more beneficial than you can possibly imagine. So, now, let's begin our exploration of this energy and the numbers within.

Numerology

Numerology, the study of the energy in numbers, is very old and began in ancient times. It is the philosophical thought that everything is created by and made up of numbers. The numbers 1-9 each have a unique energy and combine to create patterns. The universe and all things within it can be broken down into numerical patterns based on these primary numbers. These patterns determine how everything works, including us as individuals.

Each person has a numerological chart based on their birthdate and name. The pattern of numbers that occur in your numerology chart can help determine your personality, struggles, how you appear to others, best career choices, relationship needs and so on. Numerology and how the energy of numbers affect you can also be used as a divination tool. Allowing you to peer into your future and have an idea of what to expect.

Through using numerology, it is possible to map out your entire life. It gives valuable information about what you can expect throughout the stages of your life. Such as when you will have the most challenges and when you are most likely to excel in your life purpose. Numerology can also provide valuable information about how you operate in the world. Like your personality traits and patterns, how you see the world and in what ways you will find health and happiness.

Angels

The term angel, originating from the Latin word angelus, literally means messenger. Angels are the messengers of God. They are divine sparks of God's love sent to guide, love, protect and deliver divine messages to all of us.

When using the term God, I am referring to the

Creator of all things. The Source of all energy. This Source is non-denominational and is pure love. The name is not important, it is your higher-power, so you can call it whatever you are most comfortable with.

There are three types of angels responsible for assisting the earth and humanity. The guardian angels, the angels, and the archangels. Each group of angels has a certain role in life and help us in different ways. All of them are available to call on at any time.

Angels are non-denominational. They exist to help all the physical creations of God. Including us, the animals and the earth itself. They are loving and non-judgmental beings who take great joy in helping to raise the vibrations of the earth.

While you are walking your life's path and fulfilling your life's purpose, you too, are raising the vibration of the earth. Each time you help the planet or one of its inhabitants you are helping the angels raise the earth's vibration. So, in turn, the angels take great joy in assisting and supporting you. Ultimately it is a synergistic relationship of helping each other.

ANGEL NUMBERS

Angel numbers are very special signs from the angels. As each number carries a divine message that will inspire, encourage, guide and support you along your life path. They are a form of communication from our angels and they work in a similar manner to numerology; except they are easier to interpret and understand. By learning about these numbers, you have a very powerful tool for connecting with the spiritual and receiving messages from the angels.

Introduction to Angel Numbers

Angel numbers are the numbers we encounter in our everyday life except these particular numbers are sent to you by spirit and carry a divine message. Like numerology, angel numbers are used by identifying the energy in the number and applying it to our lives and our current situation. The study of numerology can get a bit complicated and needs a lot of training. Whereas angel numbers are simple to learn and understand. You can use them daily, even multiple times a day, for guidance, support, to answer your questions and communicate with the angels.

Instead of identifying numbers based on your name or date of birth and using those numbers to determine your personality and how your life will play out as numerology does, you can use angel numbers to easily and effectively communicate with angels and receive their messages of love, guidance and support. There is no specific formula to use, it is as simple as seeing the numbers and finding your message.

So, there is not much you need to learn to benefit from angel numbers. All you need to do is be aware of and take notice of them. This book will help you receive your own personal messages and help you understand what these messages mean.

CHAPTER TWO
WHY ANGELS USE NUMBERS

A ngels send numbers to us as signs that they are active in our lives and to pass on guidance, love and support. They are an easy way to stay in touch with your spiritual side and are extremely helpful as you walk your spiritual journey. The angels love to help and support us. When you become open to their assistance miracles can and will begin to occur in your life. But why do they use numbers to communicate with us? Why not just talk to us? To understand this, we need to start at the beginning.

VIBRATIONS

As you know, everything in the universe is made up of energy. All things moving and vibrating at different rates. The rate at which energy moves is known as vibrations or vibes for short. All things have a vibrational frequency, from the food we eat to the atoms that make up our physical bodies. Even our thoughts and emotions each have a unique vibrational frequency.

Vibrations are dynamic. The rate at which the vibrations resonate can be influenced and changed by the energy it is exposed to. Therefore, the energy you are exposed to will have an effect on your vibes and your energy will affect the vibrations around you.

Our thoughts and feelings influence our overall vibrations and the energy around us. Positive thoughts and feelings have higher vibrational frequencies and, in turn, negative thoughts and feelings have lower vibrations. The food we eat also impacts our vibrations. Fruits and vegetables have high vibrations whereas highly processed food has low vibrations. The energy around us and from other people creates changes in our vibrations. Being with positive, happy and caring people will raise your vibrations and being around negative, angry or unhappy people will lower your vibes. And vice versa, your energy can affect the vibes of the people around you.

You can see how powerful of a force energy and its vibrations have in our lives. But it isn't just the physical world that is made up of energy, the spiritual world is too. Just as in the physical world, all things spiritual have a vibrational frequency. Divine spiritual beings, who are not restricted by space and time nor by a physical body, have very high vibrations. The more divine the being the higher the vibrations. The lower and negative beings often referred to as demons or evil spirits have very low vibrations. Once again, the lower the being is the lower their vibrations are. While the earth and those of us in the physical realm resonate somewhere in between. Some of us higher and some of us lower.

To communicate with those in the spiritual realm it is necessary to create as much of a vibrational match as possible between us and them. This means if you want to hear the messages from your angels you need to raise your vibrations, in turn, the angels will have to lower theirs. This creates a pathway for angels to send their messages and for us to receive them. It is like being in a tall building with two separate elevators. You are on a floor near the bottom and the angels are up on a floor near the top. Your elevator will only go so high and the angel's elevator will only go so low. Keeping you separated. To talk to the angels, you need to ride your elevator up as far as it will go, while your angel rides their elevator down as far as it will go. Hopefully, now you are close enough to hear your angel talking. To be clear, the angels always hear us, as does God. This energetic matching only needs to occur so we can more clearly receive their messages. Not the other way around.

Although this vibrational matching is possible and does happen quite often, it can be problematic. After all, when we are most in need of love and guidance our energy gets very low. Depression, anxiety, grief, uncertainty and doubt are just a few of the emotions and thoughts we have that lower our vibes. As such it creates a sort of energetic wall between us and the angels. Or in the elevator analogy, keeps your elevator from going up as high. Making it difficult to receive the angel's love, support and guidance when you need it the most.

Angel Numbers Are Easy

Having a relationship with angels and communicating with them effectively takes daily effort and years of practice for most of us. Angels are purely spiritual beings, conversely, we are a combination of spiritual and physical. Although our spiritual side can vibrate at quite a high frequency, our physical bodies create a restriction. Angels can only lower their vibrations so much as well. So, creating an energetic match can be challenging and even impossible at times.

Not to mention, the physical world surrounds us with a lot of low vibrational energy. We are more likely to encounter people who are focused on the physical world rather than the spiritual. These physical experiences, our world is so focused on, takes our attention away from the spiritual. Since the spiritual is soft and subtle like a whisper and the physical world surrounding and overpowering us at times, it only takes a day or two of not actively working on your spiritual connection, to bring your vibrations down and make it quite difficult to hear your angels.

So, angels work around this energetic issue by using numbers. Numbers are an easy way to get your attention because they are everywhere. All around us - pretty much all the time. Every time you go to the store everything has a numerical value. Billboards, clocks, houses, license plates, street numbers. The time on your phone and how charged your battery is. Even the channels you watch on tv, the season and episode of that show you are watching or the pages in the book you're reading. You are exposed to numbers almost constantly. Take a look around you right now. Look at your phone, computer or the device you are reading this book from. Look around the room you are in. Notice how many numbers are surrounding you at this very moment.

Numbers are so prominent in our lives that we can see them regardless of how high or low our energy is. Or even what state of mind we're in. Angel numbers are a connection between the physical and the spiritual. They transcend the need for high or low vibrations. As such, these numbers allow the angels to communicate with us anytime. Even feelings of depression, anxiety grief and negativity don't stand in the way of seeing the numbers around you. All you need to do is be aware and willing to accept the message.

CHAPTER THREE
WHERE ANGEL NUMBERS COME FROM

As the name implies, angel numbers contain messages primarily from the angels. Like I mentioned in the first chapter there are three kinds of angels who assist the earth and humanity. They are the guardian angels, the angels and the archangels. Yet there are times when you may receive an angel number message from a spirit guide, your higher-self or even sometimes from an ascended master or saintly being.

Perhaps the term spirit numbers would be a more accurate name for these numbers. However, the word angel brings feelings of positivity, joy and love. And, ultimately, that is what these messages are; a way for the spiritual realm to provide you with uplifting, positive, joyful and loving support and guidance. So, we'll keep the name angel numbers.

Most of the time you will receive angel number messages from your guardian angels. Everyone has at least one guardian angel and most of us have two or even more. Your guardian angels have been with you since the moment you were conceived, and they will stay with you until you die. Your guardian angels are here to assist you along your life path, to guide you, and to protect you.

In addition to your guardian angels, the angels often send angel number messages as well. This group of angels is known simply as angels, but that can be confusing, so, for now, let's call them the universal angels. Because they cover every possible range of need we may ever possibly have.

The universal angels have many duties, one of them to help and assist the guardian angels. As a matter of fact, guardian angels are a specific kind of universal angel. There are an endless number of universal angels who specialize in different areas of life. Some universal angels work with those who are ill, others work with those who seek abundance and prosperity, some angels specialize in helping people with their life purpose. Others help the earth or the earth's animals. There are vast armies of angels who specialize and assist in every possible area of life.

Overseeing the universal angels are the archangels. Archangels are the managers of the angels and their primary duty is to make sure everything is running smoothly in the angelic realm. The archangels also specialize in certain areas of life. When we need extra divine assistance, the archangels are available to call on. An archangel may send you an angel number message when you have called on them, at times when you are especially blessed or when you need their specific divine powers.

In addition to your guardian angels, who are specifically assisting you, there are also your spirit guides. Although spirit guides are not angels they can and will send messages through angel numbers. Spirit guides are those who were once human and have crossed over and taken on the job of watching over someone and guiding them spiritually. Your spirit guides are usually friends, family or ancestors who have a connection to you and are now watching over and helping you along your spiritual journey from the other side.

There are times when you may receive an angel number message from an ascended master or a saintly being. If you have a special connection with an ascended master or have called upon a saint for assistance, the message you receive may be coming from them. The angel number 33 is the number for ascended masters. And when you see any number with a 3, you are being told that an ascended master is with you and assisting you. If that connection is strong there is a good chance some of your messages may be that ascended master communicating with you.

Angel numbers may also come from your higher-self. Your higher-self is the purely spiritual side of you. Unrestricted by the limitations of the physical body, your higher-self is able to guide and assist you along your life path. Your higher-self is fully aware of your needs and the journey you are meant to take in this lifetime. It is very likely your angel number messages are coming from the one who knows you best: yourself.

The angels, archangels and all other spiritual beings are required to abide by the law of free will and they will not interfere in your life without your permission. Be sure to let them know you are open and willing to receive and thank them often for their assistance.

CHAPTER FOUR
WHICH NUMBERS ARE ANGEL NUMBERS

After learning about what angel numbers are and where they come from, many people ask, how do you know the difference between an angel number and any ordinary number? The answer to this is much easier than you may think.

The angels use angel numbers as an easy way to get our attention so they can pass on messages and guidance. They are not meant to be confusing or difficult to receive. Rather they are meant to be simple and apparent. Even so, it does take some effort on your part to ensure that you are receiving divine guidance and not attributing meaning to any arbitrary number. It begins by learning to trust yourself and have faith.

When you learn to trust yourself and use your intuition angel numbers will be apparent and even obvious to you. Have faith that the angels are helping you to identify the numbers that are important. By doing so, you really have no reason to doubt yourself or your feelings about which numbers are angel numbers.

Angel Numbers Stand Out

Identifying angel numbers is as simple as noticing numbers that stand out to you. If you see a number or sequence of numbers that stands out in any way, you are receiving a message from the spiritual realm. The number may be a different color, it may be the one number in a sequence of numbers your eyes fixate on, or it may the same number repeated in a sequence. Often it is a number that you uncannily keep seeing over and over. If any number gets your attention, stands out in any way, or makes you think "that's odd" or "I wonder," you can be certain you are seeing an angel number.

This number will continue to appear until it gets your attention. You may see it one time and realize it is an angel number or the angels may show it to you repeatedly until you "get the message." Many times, the spiritual appears in 3s. If you see a number 3 times within a relatively short period of time it is likely to be an angel number.

Remember, these numbers appear anywhere and everywhere. Including clocks, license plates, signs, street numbers, addresses, store receipts - anywhere you look. It is common for the spotting of these numbers to occur several times in a short period of time making it obvious that something is up and provoking a thought or feeling within you.

For example, one day as I anxiously waited at a stop light, I looked down and saw the time was 2:22. As my eyes moved away from the clock, they focused on the odometer which said I had driven 222 miles since I last reset it. Just as I began to think "this is odd," I looked directly up at a gas station sign which read, unleaded gasoline - $2.22 per gallon. As you can imagine, all this occurring within seconds caught my attention. I continued to drive to my destination and saw the number 2 on just about everything. I remember laughing and thinking to myself, either this is a message or the number 2 is the most common number ever!

Angel numbers may not always come that quickly or be that obvious. But they will stand out and catch your attention. That is if you're paying attention. The more you pay attention and seek the guidance of your angels the more often you will see angel numbers and the more obvious they will be to you.

LISTEN TO YOUR THOUGHTS AND FEELINGS

What matters most, when it comes to seeing an angel number, is how it makes you feel, what it makes you think and what your intuition is telling you. There are people who can hear the voices of angels outside of themselves. However, most of us don't. Even those of us who do, don't hear angels that way all the time.

Angels can't just pop into the room and start up a conversation. At least not in the traditional sense. Angels are not physical - they are pure spirit. They don't have vocal cords to talk with and they don't have eardrums to hear with. So, they can't talk to us in the physical manner we are used to. They can, however, as long as we are open to it, put thoughts in our heads and they can create feelings in us.

To communicate with angels and understand their messages you must learn to listen to and hear your thoughts and recognize what you are feeling. Humans tend to struggle with this at first because we have gone so long learning to dismiss out of the ordinary thoughts and ignoring feelings. But it is through thoughts and feelings that the angels will primarily talk to you.

When it comes to angel numbers, these thoughts and feelings will not only let you know that you are seeing an angel number, it is also a very valuable way to understand the message. We'll delve into understanding the message a little later.

When you see a number and have thoughts like, "I think that is an angel number," or "Is that an angel number?" There is your answer. It is an angel number. The thought or questioning of the number is just another way the angels help you notice the signs. They put an angel or spirit energy in the number you're looking at. When you sense that added energy you take notice of it. So, if you see a number, it stands out to you, and you have a thought including "angel" or "angel number" that is the angels communicating with you. They are letting you know, that number, is important for you.

The same goes for feelings. If you just have a feeling that a number is an angel number, it is. The angels are communicating with you not only by showing you the number but also through the feeling. If seeing a number brings feelings of comfort, joy, peace, love or calm it is also a clear indication you are seeing an angel number. Messages from angels are always positive and have a benefit. So positive, good feelings often correspond with seeing an angel number. Even numbers that provide a caution or warning will feel positive, loving and nurturing.

When it comes to angels, it is very important to pay attention to what is going on within you. Thoughts, feelings and your gut are very valuable communication tools. So don't just dismiss them thinking it's coming from your own mind. An angel could be talking to you.

CHAPTER FIVE
TYPES OF ANGEL MESSAGES

Now that you know what angel numbers are, where they come from and how to identify them; what happens next? Why the fun part of course. Getting angel messages. There are three types of angel number messages you might receive depending on your situation and what is going on in your life. Knowing the type of message you are receiving is helpful for determining how to interpret the number and figure out what the angels are telling you.

GENERAL ANGEL NUMBER MESSAGES

Most people use and are most familiar with, what I call, general angel number messages. General messages are the overall general message that each number has, based on the energy it resonates with. They are the easiest to use and understand and are very common, especially when starting out. General messages usually help with things like; letting you know if you are on the right path or if you need to do something a little differently. They are often meant to remind you that you are loved and supported by the angels. General angel messages are meant to guide, inspire, support and advise you.

General angel messages are very simple. You see a number, it stands out to you and you figure out your message based on the energy of that number. Every angel number carries the message that the angels are assisting you and the reminder to pray and ask for help if you need it. Other than that, each number has its own unique energy and carries several possible messages.

To know the meaning of a number and get the general message you need to learn it. As each number 1-9 and 0 carries its own unique energy. And it is the energy each number resonates with that determines what message the angels want you to have.

Although it is all well and good to have to learn and remember the meaning of the numbers to get the message, most people don't have the time to do the research and memorize it all. So I created the guide in the second half of this book to make that a bit easier. You can easily look up your numbers, learn about the associated energy and get the primary messages of that number. You can also visit my blog at sarahdawntunis.com/angel-numbers. From there, it's up to you if and how much detail you memorize.

Direct Angel Number Messages

Once you get more familiar with angel numbers,

you may notice certain numbers appear directly addressing what you are thinking about or feeling. You may see an angel number soon after asking a question or talking to the angels. Or you may be wrestling with a tough decision and see an angel number every time it weighs on your mind. These types of angel numbers are direct responses from the angels. I call them direct angel number messages because they occur in direct response to you, rather than out of the blue or seemingly randomly the way general angel messages tend to do.

The example I shared in the last chapter about seeing the number two is an example of a direct message. Remember how I was in the car? Well, I was driving to take care of some problem and I was feeling very anxious about it. I was concerned and nervous, wondering if it was all going to work out. As I sat at the stoplight I asked the angels to give me the strength to get through it. That is when I looked up, saw the number 222 several times, followed by the number 2 everywhere I looked. The angel number 2 is a message to have faith and that things are in the process of working out, even though we may not see any evidence just yet. Seeing those 2s instantly brought a sense of relief and I knew the angels were basically saying "No worries, we got this." This was a direct response from the angels. Occurring right after I asked for their assistance. Sure enough, everything worked out smoothly and so easily I drove home wondering what the heck I was worried about in the first place.

Direct messages often manifest when you ask the angels a question or for help and soon after see an angel number directly pertaining to your question. You may be faced with a difficult decision and ask the angels "Is this the right choice for me?" and then see the number 7. One possible meaning of the angel number 7 is the decision you are trying to make is right, so go with it because you are on the right path. Or you may see the angel number 4 telling you to take a step back refocus, get organized and evaluate your priorities before going through with any decisions.

Either way, you can see how direct messages are, in fact, a direct response from the angels. Either in response to something you are thinking about, to something you asked or to a situation you are in. Direct angel messages are a fun way to have a back and forth conversation with your angels. Ask a question, then look for a number in response. The first number you see is your answer.

Like general messages, to understand direct messages you need to know the energy of the number and its meaning. This is when it pays off to have a basic idea of each number, to carry a guide along with you, or write it down to refer to later.

Advanced Angel Number Messages

As you get to know the angels and progress along your spiritual journey you will begin to resonate at a higher vibration. Among other things, this overall higher vibration will make it easier for you to receive messages from your angels. The synchronicities in your life will increase and that includes seeing angel numbers a lot more often. When this happens your angel number messages may get a little less straightforward.

Advanced angel number messages often show up as seeing several angel numbers in a day. Yet instead of seeing the same number repeating, you will see different, unrelated sequences of numbers. Such as every time you look at the clock all the numbers are the same. Or the receipt you got at the store was $99.99 and when you filled up your gas tank it came to $33.33 and when you got back in your car the time was 5:55. Advanced angel number messages are obvious and stand out, like any angel number, but since they are constantly changing and not the same number, the way you interpret the message is a little different.

This is when learning to pay attention to what you are thinking and how you are feeling becomes even more important. These advanced messages are usually not related to the energy in the number so much as the angel's way of getting your attention. They are related to what is currently going on in your life.

Whatever you are thinking about, pondering, wondering, working on or trying to decide is what these messages are in response to. It may be the angels letting you know they are constantly by your side or they could be giving you information about what you are trying to figure out. Most of the time they are a call to action. Either encouraging you to go in a certain direction or encouraging you to keep doing what you are doing. Depending on how you feel and what thoughts come to you will determine what these messages are related to.

Seeing angel numbers every day means you are receptive and open to receiving. Which means these numbers are a clear indication of the synchronicities in your life and your ability to manifest easily. The angels are at work in your life and are clearly letting you know. Advanced angel number messages work because you are already highly in tune to your spirituality and connection with the angels, so as long as you are able to tap into your inner-world, what these messages pertain to are usually clear and obvious.

However, seeing numbers like this and having the angels show you so often their presence in your life is a reward for your believing. Angels do not and will not prove their existence to people who doubt them. Seeing numbers in this manner means you are doing something right and the angels are giving you their approval. From there it is going to be up to you to pay attention and basically "decode" the message specific to you. These advanced messages may or may not have to do with the energy of the number you are seeing. Usually, they are more related to an overall feeling or thought you are having or the current situation you are in.

When you see advanced angel numbers, you'll need to determine what message the angels are trying to get across. The answers will depend on what's happening in your life. Each time you see the numbers take note of what you are thinking about before you see them, what thoughts pop into your head as you see them, and what have you been thinking about a lot in general. It can also relate to any questions you've asked the angels.

When writing my blog series on angel numbers, I got caught up in my everyday life and stopped writing the articles. My thoughts were "Does it really matter anyway?" "Is anyone ever going to read these?" "Am I on the right path with this or wasting my time?" Those types of ego-based thoughts.

While in this state of mind, every time I looked at the clock the numbers were all the same. Such as 1:11, 2:22, 3:33 etc. This kept happening and, of course, I thought it odd how I managed to look at the clock every time the numbers were the same for several days in a row. Then it started happening in other places too. Like the prices of gas, receipts etc... I didn't know what it meant, so I started by saying "Thank you, angels. What do you want me to know?" Every time I saw the numbers and asked the angels that question the thought about finishing those angel number articles popped into my head. Eventually, I realized the angels were telling me to get to work. The angels were guiding me to take action. To release my fears and concerns and continue working on my articles despite the doubt I was feeling.

Conversely, once I listened to the messages and got back to working on the articles, I kept seeing the numbers. Not quite as often, but still a lot. Especially while I was writing. But this time, when I saw the numbers I had a feeling of contentment. I felt so happy seeing the number that I would smile and nod. Because I knew, this time, the angels were letting me know I was on the right path. Encouraging me to continue. Notice how advanced messages can appear the same yet have very different and even seemingly opposite messages. In my case, I was seeing the same numbers, but the thoughts, feelings and circumstances were different. Therefore, the message from the angels was also different.

You can see how the situation and what is going on in your life when you see advanced angel number messages will determine what the angels are trying to tell you. Although it is necessary to look inward to understand any angel number message, it is especially important for understanding advanced messages.

CHAPTER SIX
SEQUENCES AND NUMBER COMBINATIONS

Angel numbers often appear as a sequence or a combination of numbers. Mastering sequences and understanding number combinations is like putting together the pieces of a puzzle. Generally, you want to start by looking at the meaning of each individual number in the sequence and then put those meanings together for a more inclusive, deeper meaning. Once you have done this, you can also add the digits together for even more understanding and clarification of the message.

There are times where certain numbers or combinations of numbers carry their own meaning, such as master numbers. In these number combinations, you have the option of looking at the number through several different lenses, all of which will enhance and add meaning to the message you are receiving.

Seeing one number at a time carries a lot of meaning

by itself so it is not necessary to look for additional numbers if you understand the message. However, angels use sequences and other number combinations because they stand out easily and get your attention, but also to add a more personalized meaning to the message they are sending you.

Let's take a closer look at what sequences and combinations may manifest in your life and how you can go about putting the pieces together.

Single Digit Numbers

Single digit numbers aren't sequences or combinations, but they are the best place to start. If a sequence of numbers is a complete puzzle, then each digit is a piece of the puzzle. Each individual single digit number is an angel number. So, a sequence of numbers is not an angel number, in itself, but rather several angel numbers strung together. The exception to this is the master numbers, which we will get to a little later. Each digit contains its own complete image, but when put together with other numbers creates a fuller more detailed image. Making it more personal and unique to you.

Single digit angel numbers are very powerful. Each number contains a lot of energy and several potential messages. As such, single numbers are the easiest way to receive a message from the angels. Just because a single digit appears to be simple does not mean the message is less powerful or important. Angels send angel number messages as an easy way to communicate with you, so if the message can reach you through a single digit that is what the angels will show you. It is enough of a challenge to communicate across realms, so the angels are not inclined to make the message more complicated or difficult to interpret if it is not necessary.

You are likely to see this single digit number several times. At least until you notice and acknowledge it. This is how the angels get your attention and ensure you understand that what you are seeing is an angel number. Remember, though, it doesn't matter how many times you see the number; what makes a number an angel number is if it stands out to you and your thoughts and feelings are guiding you to seek understanding.

Same-Number Sequences

You may see a single digit repeat itself in a sequence, creating a same-number sequence. The angels will send this kind of angel number sequence for a couple of reasons. First, sequences of numbers catch your attention. Seeing 4:44 on the clock stands out much more than seeing a single 4 by itself or amongst many other numbers. This also emphasizes the importance of the message. In the example of 4:44, the angels are making the number 4 stand out and get your attention so you will take action with confidence.

Secondly, the energy of a number is magnified and intensified when seen with itself. Seeing 44 is double the same energy as seeing a 4 by itself. 444 has triple the four energy and so on. So, the more times you see a single number repeated in a sequence the more intense that number's energy and corresponding messages are for you.

SEQUENCES AND NUMBER COMBINATIONS

Number sequences also take on the energy of their sum. By adding the digits together, you will get another number that brings more clarification to your messages. So, the number 11 has a double 1 energy and carries the 2 energy because; $1 + 1 = 2$. The number 111 has a triple 1 energy and has the 3 energy ($1 + 1 + 1 = 3$). The number 1111 will have quadruple 1 energy and additional 4 energies ($1 + 1 + 1 + 1 = 4$).

The additional energy from adding together a sequence of numbers is a way to supplement the message and help you find increased clarity. It is not necessarily part of the primary message you are receiving, rather it is a secondary energy that serves to enhance the overall message. For example, the angel number 1 means to keep my thoughts positive. The energy of the angel number 1, to keep my thoughts positive, is the primary message - no matter how many times it is repeated. If I see the sequence 111, I can find the sum of 3 which lets me know I need to keep my thoughts positive regarding how I live my life and my spirituality. In contrast, the angel number 11:11 adds up to 4. The additional energy of the angel number 4 lets me know I need to stay positive as far as making plans and goals to achieve my life purpose.

To sum all that up (no pun intended), in same-number sequences, the single digit is your primary message. The amount of times it is repeated in a sequence and the sum of adding the numbers up serve to enhance the message and bring additional clarification.

Multiple-Number Sequences

If you see a sequence of different numbers, a multiple-number sequence, the message takes on a somewhat new meaning. This is when a sequence of numbers is just like putting together a puzzle. The easiest way to start is by finding the meaning of each individual number. Once you've done that, simply put those meanings together to create the whole picture.

For example, 12. Which has the energy of the angel number 1 meaning new beginnings are happening or about to happen in your life, to stay positive and that you are surrounded by angels. In addition, we have the energy of the angel number 2, which is a reminder to have faith and that your prayers and hard work are paying off. Put those pieces together and you have a somewhat new picture, making 12 mean, as you begin something new in your life, stay positive and keep faith in yourself and your higher power. You are being assisted by the angels.

For more clarification, you can add the digits together to find the sum. Just like we did in the same-number sequences. So, in this example, the number 12 also carries the energy of the angel number 3, because $1 + 2 = 3$. The angel number 3 means you are on the right spiritual path, to live your life with joy and optimism and that you are safe and protected. This is how you know what the message from the 12 is pertaining to. So, the message from before; As you begin something new in your life, stay positive and keep faith in yourself and your higher power. You are being assisted by angels. Is regarding your spiritual path and how you are living life.

As with same-number sequences, repeating single digit numbers within a multiple-number sequence will be intensified, because any number seen with itself always intensifies that number's energy. So if the number was 122 rather than 12, there is an increased emphasis on the part of the message telling you to have faith in yourself and your higher-power.

You can also look at multiple-number sequences of three or more digits in relationship to your past present and future. The middle number(s) relates to your present situation, the first number(s) relates to your past and the last number(s), your immediate future. As with all angel numbers, listen to your thoughts, feelings and intuition to understand how the number relates to you personally and for the current situation you are in.

Of course, for the sake of keeping this all simple to understand, I have limited the above examples to the basic energy of each number. Depending on the situation, there are several variants the angel number 12, or any number can mean for you. As you start out, be sure to keep it simple, start by looking at just one number at a time. With practice, putting together the pieces of number sequences to create a whole picture will become easier.

Ascending Number Sequences

Ascending number sequences are a sequence of numbers in numerological order. Such as 123, 234, 345 and so on. These number sequences relate to the numbers they contain, but they also carry a few other meanings that add to the message.

In general, they represent the steps we need to take

to accomplish our life purpose and spiritual journey. They are encouragement to continue taking steps forward. When you see these numbers, the angels are confirming that you are headed in the right direction and making progress. I always think of these numbers like a staircase. I am at the bottom and looking up toward the "steps" I need to take to reach the top. The ascending number sequence lets me know I am at the right "staircase" and the individual numbers give me an idea of what to focus on with each step.

If you see an ascending number sequence while you are thinking about your life course or while making a decision regarding your future, it is confirmation that your thoughts and the progress you are making is on track. Right now, your future is unknowable. However, it is fated and the thoughts you are having means you are heading in the right direction.

Ascending number sequences also mean, to make things simple and straightforward. Think of the saying, "as easy as 123." It means you might want to take a step back to gain a new perspective. Reevaluate what you are doing and figure out how to simplify things. Break it down into small easy to tackle steps. Then put the steps in order and move forward. You may also want to consider cleaning out and simplifying your physical space as well. In other words, clean out your closets, get rid of things that are taking up needless space and get organized. Anything that helps simplify your life and what you are doing applies when you see an ascending number sequence.

Perhaps most significantly, through a lot of research, experience and meditation with ascending number sequences, I have found they often appear as an affirmation of life. Many people will see these sequences after the loss or near loss of a loved one, after going through trauma, abuse or a near-death experience. They often appear after having a child, especially if there were complications or concerns about the health of the child. They will appear after any kind of massive life-changing circumstance. It can be thought of as showing up after you have been touched by death and your eyes are becoming open to the value life has. A perspective only a few of us ever really have.

These sequences tend to appear soon after the crisis while you are still feeling raw and uncertain of where your life is going. The angels put ascending number sequences before you to send comfort and let you know life is beginning anew. This is a time for you to move forward, progress and build this new life. The pain you are experiencing is part of you now and is leading you toward a new understanding of the physical world and the life it contains. Touched by the severe pain of loss and trauma the physical world can bring, you are gaining new insight and value for life. It is an affirmation that the physical life you have is a gift. Take it one step at a time.

Overall ascending number sequences mean your life is heading up. Getting better and progressing toward your life purpose and what you are meant to accomplish while incarnated in this lifetime. If you see these sequences often it means you have reached an increased consciousness and your connection to the spiritual realm and heavenly entities has reached a new level.

Descending Number Sequences

There are some who believe descending number sequences, numbers in backward order, mean your thoughts are not progressive and if you continue down the path you are thinking of, you will experience regression and backward movement on your life's path. However, that is not quite accurate.

Such a meaning for descending number sequences can be confusing and lead to concern or fear. Even if your thoughts and movement along your path is regressive, seeing a descending number sequence is going to give you an idea of what to do about it. This is because angels do not send messages that create fear and concern, they are supportive, encouraging and positive and most importantly they provide guidance. The angels will not just tell you that what your thinking is wrong, they will always include some form of guidance about what you need to do. Angel messages may point out challenges and struggles you are facing, but they also give you a push in the right direction. They do not just leave you hanging and feeling lost and confused.

So, if you repeatedly see descending number sequences, it is not so much that your thoughts and the path you are on are regressive, rather the angels are encouraging you to take a step back and reevaluate your decisions and the direction you are going. You are likely to find there is something important you missed that will help you. Going back, reevaluating and gaining a new perspective will give you insight and understanding - leading you in a more simplified and effective direction.

You may also see descending number sequences when you feel like you are not making progress or moving forward. In this case, the angels use these regressing numbers to confirm they understand how you are feeling, but they want you to keep going. Despite how you feel, you are on the right track and you have their support. So don't give up.

Also, be sure to let go of the past and release anything that may be holding you back. Descending numbers may indicate that some part of your past is keeping you from growing and progressing. Don't be afraid to face old emotions, relationships or past experiences. Cut the cords and release any parts of your past that no longer serve you or your purpose. Your past will always be a part of you, but that does not mean it should be holding you back. Free yourself from any past constraints by cleaning out and decluttering those old closets. That means both the physical and psychological closets in your life.

If you want more clarity on the meaning of descending numbers, you can look at each individual number within the sequence. The energy of the first number is where you are, and the energy of the following numbers show what steps are useful to take another look at. For example, 321 may mean you are on the right track (angel number 3), but by going back to the beginning and looking at the foundation or beginning (angel number 1) will be helpful, whereas 654 may indicate the worry you have (angel number 6) is related to your planning, organization or need to be grounded (angel number 4), so return to that stage to ensure you have a safe and secure foundation to build upon.

THE MASTER NUMBERS

There are three numbers in the world of numerology that are a bit different than the rest. 11, 22, and 33. They are called master numbers and the energy they carry is very intense. As Hans Decoz, numerology specialist since 1969, puts it:

> They are called master numbers because they possess more potential than other numbers. It is also quite challenging to "master" the powerful qualities of these master numbers - they are highly charged, difficult to handle, and require time, maturity, and effort to integrate into one's personality (2011).

In numerology, there are a few people who have master numbers in their charts. Those who do, carry this intense energy with them throughout their lives and will benefit immensely from its energy. However, if they are unable to use the energy in its positive form, master numbers tend to create a lot of challenges instead. If you want to find the numbers in your numerology chart I suggest going to numerology.com for a free report.

Although master numbers carry the energy of their respective numbers and their sum, just like any other sequence, they each also form their own unique and very powerful energy. Because of this, master numbers are not usually broken down the way other number sequences are. So, when the angels send master numbers you don't need to find the sum as in other sequences. You can if you want, but it is not at all necessary and the resulting energy is less powerful.

When a master number is seen as an angel number it works a little differently than when it shows up in someone's numerology chart. Rather than having a lifelong journey of mastering the powerful energy, angel numbers only apply to your current situation or immediate future. Angels send these special numbers when you need to take the message seriously and really try to master its energy for your current situation. Since these three numbers carry such a massive amount of energy and power, when you see one as an angel number, it means the angels have serious business for you. You need to take control of your life by working to master the energy of the number for your situation. Doing so will create a clear pathway for good things to manifest in your life.

Those who frequently see master numbers are blessed, but they have a larger life purpose and generally more challenges to overcome. They are lightworkers with a unique and often more challenging life path. Master numbers are a way for the angels to let you know that you are unique, powerful and the work you do is important. Master numbers guide lightworkers through the challenges and provide reminders and guidance along their path to making the world a better place for all.

Angels use master numbers to let you know the message is extremely important to your health, wellbeing and life path. In addition, they often appear when you are potentially headed down the wrong path or facing unnecessary and self-imposed challenges. These numbers mean, if you do not master its energy you will needlessly struggle, have challenges and find it difficult to accomplish your life's purpose. On the other hand, if you follow the guidance of the master number's energy you will accomplish great things and benefit immensely. For example, angels will send the angel number 11 to those who are unfocused, lack self-confidence and are engaging in self-sabotaging behaviors. In which case, learning to master positive thinking will turn things around and set you down an abundant path.

This is because, unlike other numbers, master numbers have a duality. They can be a blessing or a curse (so to speak). To benefit from their energy, you must learn to harness and master it, which results in blessings and miracles along your path. Yet, if the message from a master number is not taken seriously, life may take a challenging turn and throw you from your purpose. The curse being challenge and struggle. So, it is imperative that you pay attention to these messages from your angels and learn to harness its power.

CHAPTER SEVEN
RECEIVING ANGEL NUMBER MESSAGES

Whether you are new to angel numbers or have been seeing them for some time now. You may be wondering how to increase the amount of angel number messages you receive. All you really need to do to receive angel number messages is to be aware of the world around you and pay attention, but there are a few things you can do to get even more assistance from the angels. By using the techniques in this chapter, you can increase the amount of angel numbers you receive and get deeper and more powerful messages.

Angel numbers are naturally occurring divine instances, so you don't need to force trying to receive them. As a matter of fact, attempting to force it will likely result in creating blocks in your psyche and prevent the messages from coming through. When it comes to communicating with angels the best thing you can do is relax and believe. Then use these techniques to help you achieve a deeper connection with the angels and receive angel number messages whenever you need them.

Pay Attention

First, learn to pay attention to your surroundings. If you are completely oblivious to what is around you, there is no way you will be able to see angel numbers. So, take the time to look up and look around occasionally. The more you do the more opportunities you give yourself to notice the signs around you.

Paying attention to what is around you is the best way to ensure that you are receiving angel messages, of any kind. If you go through life with blinders on, going about your day to day life, as usual, you are likely to miss the subtle spiritual messages that the angels place along your path. The more you practice being aware of what is around you the more you will notice angel numbers and other signs of angels.

Remember, the physical world is around you all the time and you are in a physical body. Which means your day to day physical life is always present and can easily take over your conscious mind. The spiritual, however, is within you and is much easier to forget about if you are not paying attention to and actively seeking to nurture that side of you. Your spirit is strong, but it is up against the power and influence of many.

Even on your busiest days, be sure to take some time out to really pay attention. Look around, be in the moment and get in touch with your spiritual nature.

JUST ASK

Angels are governed by the law of free will. This means they cannot assist, help or interfere in our lives without permission. Angels can put numbers injected with special energy along your path, but if you choose not to see them or take notice of them, there is nothing the angels can do. That is your choice and entirely up to you. The angels are not offended by either choice you make. They respect and appreciate the law of free will and respect and appreciate when we use it. So the choice is entirely yours. No harm, no foul.

However, the angels really love to be active in our lives and help whenever possible. When you do ask for their assistance they are happy to help as much as you are willing to receive. When you ask the angels for assistance you are giving them permission to interfere, the angels are then free to assist you. This will create the possibility of receiving many more angel numbers appearing along your path. It especially opens the door to receiving direct and advanced angel messages.

Let the angels know you are open to receiving their guidance through angel numbers. You can ask the angels a specific question or for guidance in general. Or you can ask the angels to send you angel messages more often through angel numbers. You can also ask them to help you notice, receive and understand the messages.

As a matter of fact, you can ask the angels anything you want, or you can just sit in meditation and allow the angels to hear what is in your heart. No matter how you go about it, by asking the angels to assist, you are opening the gates for their love and guidance to pour through to you.

Raise Your Vibes

In my opinion, one of the best aspects of angel numbers is how they allow the angels to reach us even when our vibes are low. As someone who personally has struggled most of my life with depression, anxiety and negative thinking, angel numbers reaching me in times of need changed my life. Although angel numbers can transcend the need to always have your vibrations high, it still pays to raise them as much as possible. The higher you can raise your vibes the easier it is for the angels to reach you and the easier it is for you to understand the message.

There are many, many benefits to having a high vibrational frequency. Including attracting positive things to yourself, feeling good and being able to receive more guidance and support from the spiritual realm. Anytime you want to communicate with the angels you can increase the frequency and intensity of the message by raising your vibrations first.

One of the best ways to raise your vibrations is by focusing on positive thoughts and what you are grateful for. Use meditation and positive affirmations to raise them even higher. Visualize what you desire and imagine the angels are surrounding you and holding you in their loving embrace. Anything that makes you feel good, calm and relaxed will increase your vibrational frequency. Try taking a bath with candles and lavender essential oil or listen to your favorite song.

Conversely, negative thoughts, feelings or doubts will lower your vibes and put a barrier between your angels and you. So do what it takes to create a good positive atmosphere. Use faith and hope to ensure your message comes through clearly and concisely. If you find yourself struggling with negativity, talk to the angels about it. Talk to them the way you do a friend or loved one. There is no one you can trust more with your thoughts and feelings than your own angels. Plenty of times I have been flooded with angel numbers and other signs that bring comfort and reassurance after a good heart to heart with my angels.

Don't stop at raising your vibrations just for communicating with the angels, it really pays to keep those vibes high all the time. Take care of yourself physically, psychologically, emotionally and spiritually. Create balance in all areas of your life. Take time to play and enjoy yourself and actively work toward your dreams every day. Whenever you feel bad, have a bad day or find yourself stuck in negative thinking, say to yourself: "How I feel is important. I deserve to feel good." Then do what it takes to feel better.

By taking at least a little time every day to focus on taking care of yourself and your needs you will ensure you have a continual state of high vibrations. Resulting in easier angel communication and a better quality of life all around.

Think About Angels Often

An easy and effective way to enhance communication with the angels is to simply think about them. The more you think, read, or talk about angels the more present they will feel in your life. Once again, talk to your angel as a friend sitting next to you. Tell them your thoughts, your concerns, your questions and your celebrations. Include the angels in all aspects of your day to day life. Including the good, the bad and even the mundane.

Why stop there? Don't just talk to them, make the angels a part of your daily life. Invite them into your life. Include them in your decisions and ask for their help when you need it. Be sure to thank them often and tell them about what makes you happy and what you are grateful for. The angels love to listen, and they love to celebrate with you.

Don't be surprised if you see an angel number immediately after or even during a conversation with your angels. Thinking about and talking to angels raises your vibrations and thins the veil between you, making communication much easier. And in my experience, angels are much more talkative then most of us imagine.

So, keeping angels in your thoughts will help to raise your vibrations and will enhance the relationship you have with them. You have your very own angels always by your side ready to listen and guide you every step of the way. And honestly, what can be better than having a loving and unconditional friend on-call every moment of every day?

BE OPEN TO RECEIVING

If you want to receive messages from the angels, you must be willing to receive them. It may sound obvious, yet this one is difficult for many people. It is especially difficult for those of us who are usually focusing on and helping others. A lot of us have learned how to give and take care of others, yet we struggle with asking for help or allowing others to give to us. But if you want to receive messages from the angels you have to be open and willing to get the message.

As with all things in life, balance is necessary when it comes to giving and receiving. So many of us dedicate our time and effort to helping others. Be it others at work, in our family or our friends and neighbors. Yet we have a hard time accepting assistance. Unfortunately, as altruistic as this way of life may seem, it is actually quite harmful on many levels. But it especially makes it difficult and even impossible for the angels to reach you and send their messages. It is like someone trying to hand you a letter, but you keep refusing to take it.

Practice receiving in your daily life. Remind yourself often that it is just as important to receive as it is to give. You are important and deserve happiness too. Get into the habit of good daily self-care and asking for help. If someone offers to help you with something, accept it - let them help you. Although it may feel a bit uncomfortable at first, remember, it is essential to your spiritual growth. There are many gifts God and his angels have for you, it is only by opening your heart to receive that these gifts can reach you.

Believe

The most important thing you can do to receive angel messages is to believe. Believe in the angels and believe that angels are there to help and guide you. Believe that the angels love you and care about you and will do whatever they can to help you. Believe in miracles. Believe with all your heart.

Do not ask the angels to prove their existence by sending angel numbers. Angels have no need to prove themselves to anyone. As such they will not send any kind of sign or message or anything else to prove they exist. Rather angel numbers are a reward for those who already believe. Your belief and faith in the angels are what fuels their messages. So, the more you believe in them, the more messages you will receive.

This is not to say you can never doubt their existence or doubt your spirituality. The angels know and understand that doubt is part of the human existence. In fact, in times of doubt, you may see angel numbers as a reminder that the angels are there for you. If you are going through a challenging time and feel doubt, ask the angels to send reassurance and guidance. They will be more than happy to send an angel number message – especially if it will help tip the scales of your doubt back into full belief. However, this is a very different situation than someone asking the angels to send a number to prove the angels exist at all.

When it comes to receiving angel messages, remember, it is not hard and is not something you need to force. Angels are the messengers of God, they are here to communicate with us. Which makes it a natural and divine occurrence. Meant to be. The biggest obstacle we face is learning to believe and accept what the world has taught us is impossible. By now you know, once we are no longer restricted by living solely in a physical world, nothing is really impossible.

CHAPTER EIGHT
UNDERSTANDING YOUR MESSAGES

The messages angels send through angel numbers go much deeper than simply looking up the meaning of a number. The numbers you see are just a starting off point. A way to point you in the right direction. Angel numbers are one of the easiest ways for the angels to send us messages and, as such, they are also very basic messages. They are simply signs from the angels to let you know they are around you, love you and to guide you. Simply put, the angel number is not much more than just an attention getter to guide you in the right direction.

The second part of this book contains a guide to the energy and messages of the basic angel numbers. This guide is designed to help you easily find the energy of each number and determine what the message may be. However, these possible messages are not all-inclusive, they are only meant to guide you toward an understanding of what the angels really want you to know. Although you can get a basic idea of what the angels are telling you by looking it up in a guide, if you really want to get the deeper and more personal meaning you will need to take the extra step to figure it out. Ultimately you are the only one who knows what your message really means.

I remember when I first began learning about angel numbers and angel messages. I found myself confused and struggling to understand what the angels were telling me. It seemed the more angel numbers I saw, the more confused I felt about what they meant for me. What am I supposed to get out of this message? How does the message of this number apply to me right now? Do the messages of this number mean the same thing as it did last time I saw it? Questions like this were more dominant than any understanding of what the angels wanted me to know. As so often happens, the more I questioned what was happening, the more confusing it got. So much so, I began wondering if the numbers I saw were in fact angel messages at all.

Many people begin their journey with angel numbers because they have seen the power of these signs in their own life. These synchronicities lead them to believe and see that it is more than just a coincidence. This is because they have witnessed the miracle of opening their eyes, hearts and minds to the existence of angels and realizing, we are not going through this journey alone. When we begin the search for a deeper relationship with the angels, thoughts of doubt, uncertainty and not "getting" the message are normal - but it can get the best of us. The problem is this uncertainty can lead to doubt and giving up entirely.

I consider myself lucky. My angels wouldn't let me

give up. As a result, I have spent the last several years researching, meditating and communicating with angels about what angel numbers mean. Do I always understand the message behind every angel number I see? No, I don't. But I do know, many times, those numbers I don't get right away are my most important messages. Certainly, worth the time it takes to figure out.

This chapter includes everything I have learned along the way about understanding what the angels are saying with angel numbers. As with most things spiritual, it is not as easy as what you see is what you get. Spirituality is about reaching beyond the physical and allowing yourself to be open to believing. Believing without the evidence of the physical world takes practice and getting used to. But with a bit of effort and the desire, it is within the reach of everyone.

The following techniques may come easily to you or they may take a bit of time and practice to really get the hang of. Be sure to treat yourself with love and understanding as you begin this journey. If one technique does not help you find answers, try another and keep coming back to each one. With experience, it gets easier and knowing what your messages are will become more intuitive.

Spiritual Work Takes Action

One of the most important things to remember as you venture along your spiritual journey is: spiritual work takes action. No matter what kind of spiritual work you are doing it requires actively working on it. Receiving, and especially understanding your personal angel number messages is no exception.

We exist in a physical world surrounded by physical and material things. Our day to day lives are full of activities, problems and experiences that help us to survive in that physical world. Additionally, most people around us are not in touch with their spiritual sides. The energy, advice and interactions we have with most people focus on the physical world, physical goals and physical responsibilities. Spirituality gets left in the dust of our physical and material ambitions, making it very easy to neglect or even forget about. Unless you are actively working to be in touch with your spiritual side and with the spiritual realm it becomes too easy for it to fall out of your conscious awareness and forget the benefits a daily spiritual practice brings. Take time every day to nurture your spiritual side, and remember, despite the physical body and world we live in - we are spiritual beings.

Action simply means to do something. Starting with listening to your intuition. Meditation, setting intentions, praying, talking to your angels, reading, using positive affirmations and working toward your life purpose are all active ways to work on your spirituality. The more in touch and aware you are with the spiritual the more angel numbers you will see and the more you are going to know what those angel numbers mean for you.

You have the choice to look up a number and see it's meaning to understand how it applies to you, that is certainly taking action. However, if you really want a deep and more precise understanding of what the angels want you to know, you need to take additional steps to obtain that understanding.

To be clear, I'm am not talking about hard work or buckling down to become a guru and expert on all things spiritual. Action can be as simple as closing your eyes and asking for more guidance or it can be as complex as meditating for hours and reading every book you can find on the subject. Spirituality is an extremely personal experience, different for each one of us. No matter which way you go about it though, spiritual work should be easy, calming and joyful. Serving to enhance your life and your soul.

The Meaning Behind the Number

As I have said, there is much more to angel numbers than just an overall message covering all the people who see that number all the time. The real meaning lies within you. After all, it is a personal message between you and your angels. No one else is privy to this information unless you tell them about it. So, there is simply no way you can look through a pre-written guide and really understand what your message is. In fact, you may not come to fully realize the message for days, months or even years later.

A few years ago, as I was just beginning my journey with angel numbers, I was going through a tough time. All I could think about was money and how I would stretch my last dollars until the end of the month. Would I be able to make the food we already have be enough? Will the kids need something that I can't afford? These thoughts had felt overwhelming for days. The money we had coming in was not covering all our needs and I was very worried, to say the least.

I ended up going to the store to buy a few groceries

with my last bit of money. As I got into my car to go home I began to cry and think "there is no way this will be enough." But, just as the tears welled up in my eyes and began to fall down my cheek, I looked across the street and saw the number 66 on an apartment. The number was big, black and bold. It stood out more than any of the other numbers around it. I wiped the tears from my eyes and looked down at the clock; it read 6:06 pm. At the time I didn't know what the number 6 meant, but I could feel I was receiving a message.

I went home and immediately began doing research on the number 6. I found out the message was telling me not to worry about my physical and material needs because they are being taken care of. I was being guided to focus on my faith and spiritual needs and let God and the angels take care of the rest. The message really hit me as being very extraordinary given my situation. So, I took the message and followed through. What else could I do anyway?

Believe it or not, we got through the month with no problems. I didn't get any more money, but somehow every night we had enough food for dinner. No matter what it was, we somehow just had everything we needed.

As you can see from my experience, the message came from my own thoughts and feelings. First, I saw the number 66 and had a feeling that it was more than a random address on an apartment building that I happened to catch a glimpse of at exactly 6:06 pm. This feeling led me to research and look through several guides and find the meaning was directly related to what I was thinking about.

In this example, it was easy to identify what the message was related to. My worry and concern about money. I was, after all, sitting in the car crying about it when the numbers appeared. However, the not so obvious part of the equation - this was the very experience that led me to learn as much as possible about angel numbers. By following the guidance to have faith and focus on my spiritual side, I was led to create this book years later. If you ask me today, I will tell you, the most important aspect of that message was telling me to focus on the spiritual. Doing so propelled my life into a new, unexpected and very rewarding direction.

Angel numbers often appear as we are thinking about something the message relates to. So, when it comes to understanding the meaning behind the number, you really want to pay attention to what you were thinking and feeling around the time you saw the number. What have your primary thoughts been leading up to seeing the number?

Also, pay attention to what "pops" into your head when you see the number. Perhaps you see the number 9 and immediately begin thinking about a close friend. Follow up with that thought and call your friend. Since one meaning of the angel number 9 is a close friend or loved one needs your help, that thought may just be leading you to the message of the number.

You may also find it helpful to look at what your focus has been on lately in general. Or even what you have forgotten to focus on. There have been many times I've seen an angel number and was unable to identify how that number relates to my thoughts and feelings at the time. Usually, this occurs because the message is about what I am intentionally not thinking about. Remember the example earlier when I was talking about advanced angel number messages? How when I began working on my angel numbers blog I began to lose my focus and forget about it until I started seeing repeating numbers every time I looked at the clock? That is an example of when the angels will send angel numbers to remind you of something you are not focusing on but should be.

Getting the Deeper Message

There are times when you will see an angel number and know exactly what the message is. Other times you will be able to look the number up, read through the various possible meanings and "get" the message. Such as the when I saw the repeating number 6. As soon as I learned about the energy of the angel number 6, I clearly understood what the angels were telling me. However, there will be a lot of times when it is not that clear or easy to understand what exactly the angels are getting at.

Sometimes the message you get from an angel number will only scratch the surface of the full message your angels have for you. Which is what happened in my previous example with the angel number 6. At first, it appeared to be a message telling me not to worry so much about my financial situation, but it ended up being so much more. By using the following techniques, I was led toward learning as much about angels as possible, which resulted in my starting a blog about angels and eventually this book. Writing about angels brings me more joy than I can even express. So, it is always a good idea to use the following techniques any time you see an angel number.

To really understand your message, you may need to start digging. If the message is not clear after taking inventory of your thoughts, feelings and what is going on in your life, don't give up. There are several things you can still do. Start by using all the steps listed in Chapter 7. This time, instead of focusing on receiving messages focus on understanding and clarification. Here is a quick review of those steps.

- *PAY ATTENTION*: Pay attention to what is going on around you. What is going on in your life? What is happening in the lives of your friends and loved ones? Be mindful of your thoughts, feelings and experiences in your day to day life. Look for more signs and angel numbers that bring clarification.

- *JUST ASK*: Ask the angels to help you understand. Ask for more signs that will guide you toward what they want you to know.

- *RAISE YOUR VIBES*: Make sure your vibrations are high by keeping your thoughts positive. If you struggle with understanding your angel message, do not give up or criticize yourself. Keep in mind, the answers will come when you are ready. And if you never figure out what this particular message means, it is not the end of the world. There will be more numbers and more messages in the future.

- *THINK ABOUT THE ANGELS*: Keep the angels in your thoughts. Don't underestimate the power of sitting and talking it all out with your angels.

- *BE OPEN TO RECEIVING*: Remember if you are not open to receiving, the angels can't reach you. Open your heart and make sure to create a balance between how much you give with how much you receive.

- *BELIEVE*: Practice faith and allow yourself to believe in the angels. Too much doubt and uncertainty will create a barrier between you and the angels making it difficult to clearly receive their messages.

Now, to gain an even deeper understanding or clarification of your angel number messages, intention, prayer, meditation and intuition are your best resources.

INTENTION:

Intention is simply setting your mind to do something or make something happen. Intention is a very powerful spiritual technique. It is a wonderful way to let the Universe, your angels and your spiritual guides know exactly what it is you want. Without intention, the mind tends to wonder, and thoughts are all over the place. Intention, on the other hand, creates a clear and well thought out picture so you can attract into your life what it is you really want.

Use intention to help clarify and understand your angel messages by setting your mind to receive clear messages and understanding from the angels. Say what your intention is out loud to reinforce it in both in your mind and for the Universe.

Prayer:

Prayer is the practice of talking directly to your higher power. To God. We do not pray to angels; however, angels do help carry and deliver the message to God. So, when you pray with your angels, you know what you have to say is going straight to the source. Angel numbers are most commonly known to come from the angels and they can come from any spiritual being assisting you. Yet ultimately, regardless of who delivers your messages, they are all coming from God. So you do not need to limit yourself to just asking the angels to help understand your angel number messages. Asking God through prayer is the most powerful way to ensure you are getting the right message delivered to you and from you by the right spiritual being.

Use prayer to talk to God and directly ask for clarification. Ask God to send signs and messages in any form that will help you connect to your spiritual side. Be sure to use gratitude and thank God for the gifts he has given you, including the angels and angel numbers.

Meditation:

Meditation is the technique of clearing your mind and gaining access to your subconscious. Among many things, meditation is used for relaxation, for embedding what you want into your subconscious mind such as in guided meditation, and to help you connect to your higher-self and the spiritual realm. It is the practice of letting go of the physical world around you and opening yourself to the deeper parts of you.

Use meditation by clearing your mind and deeply focusing on the angel number and the corresponding message. When using meditation, you are letting go of the physical and mental blocks that may be stopping you from understanding your messages. It clears your mind of unnecessary clutter and opens you up to receiving clear messages. Creating a clear path for the angels to communicate with you.

Intuition:

Intuition is that part of you that softly guides and leads you in directions logic, rationality and the physical world do not always see. Often it is referred to as your gut instinct. There may be no reason for you to feel something is right or wrong, you just feel it in your gut. Intuition is direct access to your higher-self – your purely spiritual self. Your higher-self sees and knows things you do not while in the physical body and it communicates with you through your intuition.

One of the most important things you can do to understand your messages clearly and thoroughly is to use your intuition. There is a good chance you already know what the message is. Bring it into your consciousness by taking time to relax and reflect on the energy of the number and everything going on in your life. By looking to your inner-self, more often than not, you will find you know exactly what the message is.

Simple Meditation to Clarify Angel Number Messages

Anytime you want to further understand your angel

number messages do this simple, yet very effective meditation. Take some time away from your everyday busy life by finding a quiet place to sit and relax. Take a few deep breaths and set the intention to become as relaxed as possible and to communicate effectively with the angels. To further enhance the experience, you can light some candles, play soothing music and/or sit near some fresh flowers. Then clear your mind of any of your worries and focus on the angels and the angel number(s) you saw. Say "thank you, angels, for helping me understand this message you have for me."

Sit in this relaxed quiet state for a while and watch the thoughts flow by. Some thoughts will be your thoughts and your busy mind going about, as usual, just let those thoughts keep going by you. Let them gently float out of your awareness. Some thoughts you will notice are new, original and bring clarity to what you have asked the angels. Sometimes you will have a new or unexpected feeling, either by itself or associated with a thought. These thoughts and feelings are from the angels and can bring very precise and specific messages to you. They will feel like answers or even like an "ah-ha" kind of moment where you just suddenly understand how the meaning and energy of the number applies to you.

Doing this practice to communicate with angels is very effective. The more you practice this meditation and learn to separate your own thoughts from those the angels are giving you, it will become easier and faster. You will have a greater understanding of what the angels want you to know and how they are guiding you.

IS THIS MESSAGE ABOUT YOUR FUTURE?

If, after trying all the above techniques, you are still uncertain what message the angels are trying to get across to you - don't give up just yet. The angels will send messages that you aren't quite meant to understand at the moment. Rather, they are meant to prepare and guide you for what may be coming.

Spend the next few hours, days, weeks or months and sometimes even years following your heart and inner-guidance. Depending on what the angels are preparing you for determines how far in advance they will send these messages of preparation.

For example, not too long ago, I began seeing the number 5 literally everywhere. By now I am certainly aware of what the number 5 means, but I was unable to determine why the angels were showing it to me. The angel number 5 means big, life-transforming change and it is one of the angel numbers I rarely, if ever, see. It all started on May 5th, when my grocery bill was $155.55 and every day for over two months, I continued to see the number 5 and sequences of 5 on just about everything, yet had no idea why.

Then after a couple of months, I found myself in a situation where I was being thrust in a new unexpected direction. Suddenly, my life was completely changing. It's one of those changes that I really want but feels like I'm not quite ready for. It is a roller coaster of emotions, oscillating between excitement and terror. To tell you the truth, if it weren't for angel numbers, I would be afraid my life is likely to fall apart feeling concerned that I am not ready for this. However, the angels showed me the angel number 5 for so long I have had plenty of time to prepare.

It brings comfort to know the angels have my back and are supporting me through this change. It is this comfort and the knowing something was coming that gave me the courage to step out of my comfort zone and take the leap toward this change rather than cowering away from it.

So, no matter how experienced you are at receiving angel messages there are going to be times when the message is meant for something in your future. Just because you aren't quite understanding your angel number message in the moment, don't give up. With time the answer may come, and the message will be crystal clear. You can always write these numbers down and revisit them at a later time.

Where Is the Number Leading You?

If all else fails, remember, angels, use angel numbers to guide us. So, when you see an angel number and are not sure what the message is, don't stress about it. Just wait it out and see where the number leads you. Go about your day and naturally follow your intuition. See where the number and the thought of the number take you. Be on the lookout for other synchronicities such as any kind of help, miracles, lessons, signs or more angel numbers.

Perhaps the number is not a message in itself, but rather, a way for the angels to change your path and guide you in the direction you are meant to go. Your search for an answer may take you to unexpected places, such as looking up the number yet finding something else new and helpful for your current situation. Or you may turn to a friend who gives you some great advice. Or maybe you decide to stop trying to figure it out altogether and instead watch a movie or tv show that eerily relates to your life and helps solve a problem.

Even if you don't completely "get" the message, if you relax and follow your intuition you will be led to the exact place you are supposed to be. Sometimes angel numbers are put along our path to help change the direction we are going and send us toward something better and more useful. It is not always necessary to know exactly what the number means as long as it takes you along the best path. So be open to the possibilities.

Keep a Journal

I have found that keeping a journal is an extremely helpful way to understand angel messages. I recommend going out and getting a special journal that you dedicate only to your experiences with angel numbers. Keep it in a convenient place or even carry it with you so you can jot down anything, such as numbers you see and what you were thinking and feeling in the moment.

There are several ways that keeping an angel number journal can benefit and enhance your communication with the angels. Here are a few of my top reasons.

It Holds the Memory:

Whether you can't seem to figure out what your message is or if you want to go back someday and see how far you have progressed along your spiritual journey and communication with angels, keeping a journal helps you remember all the details that otherwise would slip your mind rather quickly.

Communicating with angels and the spiritual realm is similar to dreaming. In that it is very vivid and feels like the memory of it will last forever. Yet as time goes by, the memory begins to fade until it is gone. Many times, while reading my journal, I will come across something I have no memory of. Clearly, I wrote about it in my journal, yet like a dream, the memory has faded away.

This is to be expected though. Communicating with angels changes your brain waves which are the same brain waves you experience while dreaming. The brain is not wired to embed these experiences in the long-term memory. Therefore, once the experience is over the brain goes back into its usual waking pattern and the memory fades away.

Keeping a journal of your experiences will hold the memory for you so you can always return to it. You've heard of a dream journal, where people record their dreams? Think of this as your Angel Number Journal.

It Helps You Process:

As with any kind of journaling, the process of writing things down helps you think about and process what is going on. You may find writing about your experiences and thoughts while trying to decipher the meaning of your angel number message helps you discover things you never would have thought of otherwise.

It is a Form of Meditation:

Writing done without any kind of restriction, which means it is not like writing an e-mail or something for school or work for a specific purpose, is a form of meditation. It, once again, changes your brain waves and relaxes you. Giving you access to your subconscious mind. This allows you to freely obtain information that is not normally in your conscious awareness. The subconscious mind holds a lot of thoughts, feelings and desires that have an effect on our day to day life - even though we are usually completely unaware of them. Journaling can help you access and uncover these thoughts, motivations and desires. Helping you discover more about yourself and understand what your angel number messages mean.

You Might Be Able to Channel the Angels:

There are a lot of people who channel angels through writing. It probably doesn't come as too much of a surprise that I am one such person. Most of what I have learned from the angels comes from clearing my mind and sitting down with a pen and paper or at my computer and just writing whatever flows through me. Most of the time when I do this, I don't even know what I wrote until I go back and read it. You may find as you journal about your angel number experiences you will channel the angels, meaning the angels write through you. So be sure to go back and read what you wrote.

CHAPTER NINE
YOUR ANGEL NUMBERS

Most people who hear the term angel numbers think of synchronistic repeating numbers sent by angels. However, angel numbers are not limited to the numbers you see along your path. In fact, you can be the one to bring the energy of angel numbers into your own life. In this next chapter, I will go over a few cases of what I like to call your angel numbers (or my angel numbers, as the case may be) because when these numbers appear in your life they are unique and special to you.

Your angel number(s) usually appear on and off throughout your entire lifetime. These numbers have a similar reoccurring theme whenever you see them, and that theme is specific to you. Generally, they apply to your life path and are reminders to be true to yourself and use your natural talents and abilities.

Life-Long Recurring Numbers

Some people have a certain number that continues to appear throughout their life. The number begins to appear when you are young or perhaps at the beginning of a new life phase. These life-long recurring numbers are usually noticed in connection with significant people, places and things. Many people will notice all the birthdays of people they love share a common number or other significant dates such as deaths and marriages have this number. Maybe the house they grew up in, bank account numbers, phone numbers and so on all commonly have this number. These life-long recurring numbers are a consistent part of their life and hold significance for that person. This same number may also be the most common angel number the person sees.

Life-long recurring numbers are a form of communication from your spiritual guides. Whenever you see this number you are receiving confirmation that you are being watched over from the other side. If you have a life-long recurring number, it is because you are open and connected to the spiritual realm and have a deep spiritual awareness. So, your spiritual guides, be them angels or crossed over loved ones, have been able to leave little bread crumbs sprinkled throughout your life letting you know you are not alone.

The energy of this number also pertains to your life path or soul's purpose. Look at it as an energy you are meant to work with and master while in this life. It can help you determine what you are meant to do and what your underlying focus is meant to be when you make decisions, when you feel lost or confused or to help you understand what you are meant to do with your life.

Your Birthday

When you see the numbers of your birthday it is a call for you to focus on your life purpose and take some time to cherish and celebrate your life. Seeing your birthday means the angels are celebrating who you are and what you have and are meant to accomplish. The angels want you to look to your true-self with love and appreciation. Doing so, enables you to accomplish your life purpose with joy, enthusiasm and confidence. God created you perfectly to accomplish this mission, your birthday numbers remind you of this.

The angels will repeatedly send your birthday numbers when you are on track and accomplishing your life purpose. Your birthday numbers are in celebration of your achievement and success in finding and using your God-given abilities and talents. If you have recently put yourself out there by taking risks and following your heart, your birthday numbers signify that you are on the right track and the angels are celebrating and urging you to continue.

Your birthday numbers may repeatedly appear when you are feeling doubtful, uncertain and experiencing low self-confidence. The angels will send your birthday numbers as a message that you are important and perfect in the eyes of God. It is a reminder that you are made perfectly to accomplish your soul's mission. Take the time to recognize and celebrate yourself and your natural skills and talents. Remember who you are is who you are meant to be.

Your birthday numbers are also a call to step back from what you are doing and the path you are on, reanalyze and gain a new perspective. Birthdays signify the beginning of our physical lives. Likewise, your birthday numbers may be the angels letting you know, now is a good time for a fresh outlook and a new start. Be sure you're on the path to creating happiness and joy in your life by using your natural skills and talents. Take a break to get organized, reassess and make sure you are on the path you really want to be on. If you are on the right path, take the time to celebrate your accomplishments and prepare for the change your achievements will bring in the next phase of your life.

Be a Co-Creator

Your own special angel number may also be of your choosing. As with all spiritual things, angel numbers are a two-way street. To receive the energy of an angel number is not always a passive activity where we just sit and wait for it. We also have the ability to bring the energy of any number to us. The angels can send us a number as a message, but we can attract the energy of a number into our lives as well.

If you are familiar with the Law of Attraction, you know you are a co-creator of your own life. Meaning, you have a say in what happens in your life and the energy that flows through you. You can choose what you attract into your life and what experiences you will have. Angel numbers are a wonderful and easy way to help you bring certain energies into your life. The angels are very supportive of and love when we take the wheel and use angel numbers to co-create.

If you want the energy of an angel number in your life all you need to do is focus on that number. Meditate on the number and think about that number often. Use your intention to attract that number's energy into your life. With your focus on your number and its corresponding energy, you will attract that energy to you.

You can also attract a number's energy to you by using it often. Use the number in usernames and passwords or anywhere you need to come up with a number. Don't be surprised if the angels start showing your number to you. It means the angels are supporting your effort and helping you along. You may also see your number with the angel number 2. Which means the angels are letting you know your work to attract that energy is working, so have faith and don't give up.

Your Favorite Number

You may not realize it, but your favorite number is one of your angel numbers. It may be one of the most fun of all the angel numbers because you have a special and unique connection to it. Sometime in your past, you decided this particular number was your favorite. You were drawn to the number because when you thought about it, it gave you a unique feeling other numbers did not quite have.

Whatever number is currently your favorite number is a mutual attraction. Meaning you chose the number as your favorite and the energy of the number was also attracted to you. Using the Law of Attraction, your energy and the energy of that number converged and created a special connection. Hence, it is your favorite number.

Because of this mutual attraction between you and your favorite number, there are overlapping energies that explain your personality, how you see the world, your values and what your life purpose is. Read about the energy of your favorite number and see how many of the qualities and attributes of that number resonate with you on a deep level and explain aspects of your personality and how you operate within the world.

Studying and understanding the energy of your favorite number can help you determine why you make the choices you make and what makes you happy. These are the energies that will assist you the most along your life path and help you find the happiness and satisfaction you are searching for in this lifetime. Embrace these energies within you. You are likely to find them to be the easiest energy for you to master because they come very easily to you. However, if you resist these energies you may find difficulties and challenges along your life path.

Use the energy of your favorite number to guide and assist you with your soul's mission. You are very well-equipped to use these energies for lightwork. Such as helping others learn and master the energy of your favorite number or use the number's energies to heal and assist others.

Your favorite number also works as a lucky-charm or lucky-number. Over the years of having this number as your favorite, you have embedded it with a lot of positive energy. You have placed this number above all others and held it in high regard. Which results in the number having very high vibrations and positivity for you. The longer the number has been your favorite the higher vibrating and lucky the number is for you. When you need an extra bit of good luck, bring in the energy of your favorite number by thinking about it, meditating on it or using it whenever or wherever you can.

It is possible for your favorite number to change over time. As you grow and develop along your spiritual journey, your energy can change and evolve. Resulting in your resonating with another number. Changes that naturally occur depending on your life phase, life circumstance or a change in energy due to self-growth will often affect what number you connect with the most.

CHAPTER TEN
WHEN ANGEL NUMBERS STOP

What does it mean when you stop seeing angel numbers? This is a question I have heard quite a few times and there are several answers depending on the situation. It is not uncommon for angel numbers to stop suddenly after you have been seeing them for a while. Maybe the one number you have been seeing for a long time is no longer showing up or perhaps you are just not seeing repeating numbers at all. Either way, it is normal for angel numbers to lack an appearance and it is common to wonder why. What happened?

Depending on you, where you are along your life path and what message the angels have for you in the moment determines when and if you will see angel numbers. Going a period of time without seeing angel numbers is no cause for concern. But if you are asking the angels for assistance and you're not getting a response there are a few things you may want to consider.

This chapter goes over the most likely reasons for not seeing angel numbers and what you can do about it. Remember, if you find you are not receiving angel numbers, it is always helpful to go back and review the previous chapters on how to receive and understand your angel messages. Otherwise, make sure it is not due to one of the following reasons.

You Got the Message

The angels will continue to show you an angel number or sequence of numbers until they have your attention and you have acknowledged the message. Or until the message no longer applies to you. When you notice and acknowledge that the angels have sent a message, you open the gate for more messages to come. Sometimes the angels will give you a new message immediately or overlapping other messages. Yet sometimes the angels will give you time to process and follow through with a message before they send a new one. This results in a lapse of time where angel numbers just don't appear.

If you have been paying attention and working toward understanding the message and taking appropriate action, the angels will stop showing you the angel number. This is simply because you got the message. What a wonderful time to celebrate. Now the angels can send new messages to help you progress along your life path. Trust in the angels to send the next angel number when the time is right.

What to do next:

If you stopped seeing angel numbers because you

got the message, now is the time to pat yourself on the back and keep going in the direction you are going. You can always ask the angels for more guidance or to send an angel number to confirm you are still on the right path. If you just want to see numbers to be certain the angels are with you, simply ask them to send numbers as reassurance. Or you can even pick a number you want the energy of in your life and start meditating on it. No matter what, as long as you believe and are working toward your spiritual life purpose, the angel numbers will start back up again when you need them.

You're Out of Alignment

It happens to the best of us. Things are going great and then…well… life happens. Something throws you off track and the challenge gets you down in the dumps. Being worried, anxious or depressed about what is going on in your physical life can create blocks and make it hard for the angels to reach you. Also, if you are too focused on what is going on in your physical life, you will likely be less aware of your spiritual surroundings. Resulting in missed signs and opportunities.

What to do next:

If this happens don't let it worry you even more, simply follow the steps in chapter seven and be sure to take very good care of your physical, mental, and emotional health. Always remember you can call on the angels to help you with this or anything that is going on in your life. Regardless of whether you see angel numbers or not, the angels are there assisting you and waiting for you to call on them.

Not in Sync With Your Higher-self

You may become out of alignment when your decisions and choices are not in-sync with your higher-self. Your higher-self is your purely spiritual side. Like other spiritual beings it is not limited by space and time and therefore it is aware of your spiritual journey occurring before, during and after this physical incarnation. Your higher-self is acutely aware of your life purpose and what you are meant to learn in this physical life.

When you are in alignment with your higher-self and your life purpose you will feel a sense of joy and at ease with life in general. These positive feelings are an indication that you are on the right path. However, when we get too caught up in worry and the physical world we tend to make decisions that are out of alignment with the higher-self. These choices and actions create feelings of depression, anxiety and a general unhappiness or unease about life. Simply put, life feels harder and less rewarding.

In this case, it will be much harder for you to receive angel messages. Being out-of-sync with your higher-self creates blocks, negative thoughts and feelings and lowers your vibrations. Since angels are here to bring messages to guide you along your life path, if you are headed in the wrong direction it is much harder for them to reach you.

What to do next:

Take a step back, breathe and reassess what you are doing with your life. If it is not making you happy or feel good about yourself - find something else to do. Do what it takes to bring balance, joy and happiness into your everyday life. This is sometimes easier said than done, however, the rewards on every level of your well-being are worth the risk it takes to step out of your comfort zone.

Take time to meditate with the intention of connecting to your higher-self. This will open the channel for you to feel and align with your higher-self. Listen closely to your intuition because that is how your higher-self is most likely to communicate with you. Learn to block out the noise and distraction of the physical world. And be especially careful of acting upon any thoughts, feelings or words of others that tell you "you should" be doing something. Let your intuition guide you rather than trying to do and be what the physical world thinks you "should."

You're Not Paying Attention

If you are not paying attention to what is going on around you, you will miss opportunities for the angels to send messages to you. So often, we get caught up in our day to day life. Walking around with blinders on. We have so much to do and so much to worry about that we often get hyper-focused on accomplishing it all. Which results in not seeing much beyond what is in front of your face. This way of being is very unhealthy, lowers your vibrations and makes it hard to notice the subtle angel numbers all around you.

You can't ask the angels for help or to answer a question and continue with life as usual. You need to do your part. You need to follow up by really paying attention and acting upon the guidance your angels are sending you. Otherwise, it is like leaving a message for someone to call you back and then turning the ringer to your phone off. It just doesn't work, you can't receive the call if you don't pay attention to the phone the call is coming in on.

What to do next:

Practice letting go of the daily grind and give yourself time to relax and be in the present moment. Pick up your head and look around often, taking notice of the beauty all around you. Utilize the techniques included in the next chapter, Increasing Your Awareness, to train your mind and body to be more aware of your surroundings.

You're Intentionally Ignoring the Message

Wait… don't skip this section because you think it doesn't apply to you. We all experience this problem. Especially when first learning to communicate with angels. We ignore the messages and we do it on purpose. Albeit, usually not consciously. Meaning we do it without realizing we are doing it. So, at first glance you may think there is no way you are intentionally ignoring your angel messages, however, if you never tend to do this, you probably would have no need to read a book like this.

Angels communicate to us from the spiritual realm

and their messages are subtle and gentle. As you already know, you need to play an active role when communicating with angels or you may miss the signs. You may be great at paying attention but paying attention won't get you very far if you ignore or dismiss the signs you receive. Right? Makes sense.

So here lies the trouble for most of us. We have been taught that reality only exists through our five senses. That hearing voices or seeing things means you are crazy and probably need medication. That synchronicities and signs are coincidences and meaningless. If this is the way you are used to looking at and perceiving the world, you may ignore the subtleness of your angels or you may tell yourself that your thoughts and feelings are just coming from your own head.

Communicating with angels and receiving angel numbers requires us to believe and change our way of thinking. Not everything can be explained by physics or science. In fact, just in your lifetime, how many scientific facts have changed? Or remember how science was certain the Earth was the center of the universe and the sun rotated around us? Science gets things wrong and it has a long way to go before it can explain everything that happens in our physical experience. Especially since many people believe science and spirituality must be kept separate. As William Shakespeare so poetically put it, "There are more things in heaven and earth, Horatio, than are dreamt of in your philosophy." (Hamlet 1.5.167—8), the scientific philosophy has a long way to go.

We have so many more senses than just sight, sound, touch, smell and taste. Intuition is yet another sense most of us were not taught in science class. Yet it is one of our most powerful senses. Your intuition guides you through life, warns you of potential danger and allows you to communicate clearly with the spiritual realm. Learning to understand and develop your intuition is one of the most powerful tools you can give yourself.

What to do next:

Don't always dismiss thoughts or feelings or the voices in your head. Learn to discern between your own inner-voice and the thoughts the angels are giving you. That spark of light you saw from the corner of your eye may be your eyes playing tricks on you or it could be an angel. With practice and experience, you will learn to know the difference. But you must continuously keep your mind and heart open to the possibilities. No matter how strange it feels at first.

In the meantime, don't ignore or dismiss the odd things you experience or feel, because it just might be the angels talking to you. Try writing them down, meditating and asking the angels to help you determine the difference between the physical and the spiritual. When you experience something out of the ordinary or coincidental ask the angels to let you know if it was from them by sending you a sign. Then be open to receiving the sign.

The more you practice listening, seeing and experiencing the world beyond your five senses the more natural and easier it becomes to communicate with your angels and the spiritual realm.

CHAPTER 11
INCREASING YOUR AWARENESS

Except for a few lucky ones, most of us live a very fast-paced, focus-driven life. Always striving and reaching to accomplish the next task. We have so many things to deal with and focus on every single day there isn't much time left. Not even enough time to eat healthily and sleep sufficiently. Did you know according to the CDC (Center for Disease Control) 1 in 3 American adults are sleep deprived?

Many of us are so busy looking forward, reaching and striving for some future goal that each moment slips by practically out of our awareness. For those of us on the path of spiritual awakening and enlightenment, this fast-paced life is counter-productive. It lacks balance and self-care and submerges us in the lower energies of the physical world. Only serving to separate us from the spiritual world we desire to embrace. If you want to receive and understand angel messages, learning to slow down and pay attention is vital. Unfortunately, this is not always as easy as it sounds.

This chapter and the following techniques are ways to help you slow down, relax and train your mind, body and spirit to become aware of everything around you. Many of these techniques will require effort and practice, but it is well worth the time it takes to master. These techniques will help to increase your sense of joy, manage stress levels, help you be a better listener, and fulfill any role you have in life more efficiently. Be it at work, at home or spiritually. Helping you to be more well-rounded and raise your vibrations; bringing you closer to the angels.

LEARN AND PRACTICE GOOD SELF-CARE

You probably spend a lot of time taking care of other people and the things that need to get done in your life. This is important, but ask yourself; are you putting enough time into taking care of you? The key to achieving a higher vibrational frequency and being more in touch with the spiritual realm is by taking care of your whole self. As humans in a physical body, we need to learn to see and treat ourselves as a whole. Which includes nurturing our mind, body and spirit. If your body and mind are in good shape your spiritual growth will have the opportunity to soar.

Your physical body is a vessel. You need to take care of and nurture it every single day. Be sure you are eating well. Which means eating a healthy diet *for you*. Eat enough, but not too much and eat foods that nurture your body and make you feel well. Go to the doctor and get a check up to be sure you are in good health. Ask to be tested for any food sensitivities or intolerances. Then create and follow a diet that is right for you.

Shake it up. Work your physical body by getting some activity every day. Even a daily walk for 30 minutes will increase your feel-good chemicals and hormones and give you more focus and energy for other daily activities. Being physical and working up a bit of a sweat will help your body release toxins including toxins built up from stress, the environment and processed food.

Finally, take a break. Be sure to take care of your mental and emotional health as well. You can't be a mover and a shaker all the time - we are meant to rest and recharge. Take some time every day to relax, clear your mind and do something you enjoy. Try taking up a hobby, play with the kids, read a book, or enjoy a candlelit bubble bath. Whatever it is, make sure it is something that brings you peace and joy. It's okay if you don't get everything done today, some tasks will be just fine waiting until tomorrow. Learn to make yourself a priority.

Create Balance in All Areas of Your Life

Create balance in all areas of your life is something you may hear quite a bit, but what does it really mean? It is not like you can run over the nearest store and pick up a scale to measure which areas of your life are out of balance. Even if you could, how do you fix it? Once again, we have one of those suggestions that is easy for me to tell you to do but may be much harder for you to implement.

INCREASING YOUR AWARENESS

As you read through the following areas of how to make sure the important areas of your life are in balance, keep in mind, you don't have to get this right all the time, every time. Having and creating balance in your life is important, however the world we live in, the tasks we are expected to complete, the way we were raised, and how we see the world can make creating balance challenging at times.

Some areas are easy to create and maintain balance, some areas take effort and still other areas seem to fall back into old off-balance patterns easily - if we are ever able to really get them into balance in the first place. Ultimately, none of that matters, what does matter is knowing yourself and knowing what areas of your life really need the most effort to create and maintain balance. Those areas will always require a bit of work and attending to on your part and as long as you know that about yourself, you are on the right path. So do your best and strive for as much balance as possible. But, please, do not get down on yourself if you cannot get this perfect.

Here are a few areas most of us tend to get out of balance quite a bit. Put your effort into creating this balance, but as I said, it can take the rest of your life to get all these areas in balance all of the time. So try not to take on too much at once. You don't need to make sure every area of your life is in complete balance tomorrow. Having balance is a process and will need to be adjusted as life changes. So start by working on one area at a time and move on to the next when you are ready. Let your intuition guide you.

Giving and Receiving:

It is just as important to receive as it is to give. If you have a hard time receiving, you are going to create a block from receiving angel numbers, angel signs and other angel messages. Angels are here to help you, guide you, assist you and love you. If these are things you normally struggle with accepting from others, you will end up struggling to accept it from the angels as well.

Practice receiving from others as much as you give. If someone offers to help you, take them up on the offer. If you could use some help, ask for it. If someone gives you a compliment say thank you and accept their sincerity. Tell yourself every single day that you are important and deserve to be happy and successful just as much as everyone else does.

Work with Play:

Work is a necessary and important part of our physical life. And not much beats the feeling of a job well done. However, getting caught up in working and neglecting the fun side of life can lead to burn out, stress, anxiety, depression and physical illness. We've all heard the proverb and quote from the Shining: All work and no play makes Johnny a dull boy. It may be extreme, but Stanley Kubrick gives a good argument in his movie. Jack opened himself up to the forces of evil by being overly focused on work and achieving societal expectations while neglecting the needs of himself and his family.

I doubt anything like that will happen to you, just the same, be sure to balance all that work you do with a bit of fun time. All parts of you are important, not just your working and productive self. So, get in touch with and nurture your inner-child. Let yourself be impulsive and spontaneous at times. Take a vacation and enjoy life. By doing so you will find you are much more productive, satisfied and efficient in the long run.

Activities with Rest:

Work actively toward accomplishing your goals and dreams, go out and play and get enough physical activity each day to feel well. However, don't skip on the rest your mind and body need to recover, recharge and prepare for more activity. If you are constantly active without taking any time out it will be hard to see what is happening outside of your focus.

Rest often and take the time to just sit and do nothing. It would be nice if our angel numbers would ring a bell to get our attention like our phones do, but they don't. We have to be open to seeing them. The easiest time to receive a silent and subtle message is when you are relaxed and simply doing nothing much of anything. Not to mention when you're well-rested you are also more attentive during times of activity.

Healthy Restriction with Indulgence:

There are some things in life that are better to restrict rather than indulge in. Such as sugar and junk food. But too much restriction, even if it is healthy and what is best for you, can create an energy of lack in your life. So it is okay and even good for you to occasionally indulge in those things you really love. An occasional trip to the ice cream shop for your favorite creamy, sugary treat will help you feel satisfied and not so deprived. Make sure your indulgences are not harmful to yourself or anyone else, such as in the case of addiction. Otherwise, use healthy restriction most of the time but allow yourself to indulge every-so-often.

Go a step further and for everything you restrict from your life, find a satisfying, healthy indulgence. If you can't have sugar go on the search for a yummy, sugar-free tasty treat to have when you're feeling deprived. If you can't eat gluten, find a restaurant that serves great gluten-free options to be your new favorite dish. Whatever it is you need to restrict in your life, there are many options out there that can serve as a more than adequate and perhaps even better replacement. You just need to be willing to find it.

Relationships:

Create balance in all your relationships. Be them personal or professional. Relationships are a two-way street. When in a healthy relationship you are getting as much (if not more) than you are putting into it. But when relationships are off balance it eventually results in unhappiness and resentment. Neither of which are good for relationships or raising your vibrations. As human beings, we are social creatures and our quality of life is dependent on the relationships we have. Therefore, healthy and balanced relationships are essential.

There is more than enough information about how to ensure you have healthy balanced relationships to fill an entire book. However, the most important thing you can do is balance taking care of those you care about with letting them take care of you. Make sure you are getting at least as much out of every relationship that you are putting in. Have fun and spend time with your loved ones to increase everyone's emotional fulfillment. Work at a job where your boss treats you with respect and where you are well compensated for the work you put in.

Since relationships are a two-way street, sometimes, no matter how hard you try, there are people you just can't have a balanced relationship with. Those who are negative, put you down, abuse you in any way or who expect you to be there for them but are not ever there for you are harmful. Family, friends or anyone else who are unable to be supportive of you and continuously drain your energy are best to be avoided whenever possible. You can still love these people but keep them at a distance and avoid feeding into their energy drain on you.

Last, but not least, put time, energy and effort into your relationship with the angels and God. These powers are continually by your side loving you, be sure to balance that by giving back a bit of gratitude, attention and love. When it comes to spiritual guides don't underestimate the power and importance of a sincere heartfelt thank you.

LEARN AND USE MINDFULNESS

Mindfulness, the practice of being mindful, is having an awareness of everything around you and within you in the moment. It requires letting go of any thoughts about the past, the future or current concerns and worries and just being present. Being present and aware of your surroundings and what is happening only in the current moment in time. You've heard the saying, *stop and smell the roses*. Mindfulness is the practice of doing exactly that - taking the time to stop and experience the world existing around you.

Sensory adaptation is a psychological phenomenon where the body adapts to much of our sensory input by tuning it out. This process is necessary for survival in the physical world because it keeps us from becoming overwhelmed by all the sensory stimuli coming at us on a regular basis. For example, notice how you do not feel the clothes you are wearing unless you are thinking about it? Can you imagine how difficult it would be to focus on anything if you constantly felt, saw, heard, tasted and smelled everything around you? You probably wouldn't get much done. So, your brain tunes out anything it deems unnecessary, enabling you to go about your day and focus on more important things.

Sensory adaptation, though, is both a blessing and a curse. It does what it is supposed to do to help us survive, but sometimes it does the job too well. We become so accustomed to all the life around us and, in turn, so focused on our goals, responsibilities, problems and worries that we never notice what our brain is filtering out. So much beauty, experience and signs around us go completely unnoticed.

Mindfulness is intentionally giving your mind and body a break from the constant activity of day to day life and noticing what you normally tune out. It increases relaxation, creates a sense of calm and gratitude and provides an entirely new perspective of what it means to live in the physical world. With a daily mindfulness practice, you will increase your awareness of what is around you in any given moment. It will raise your vibrations and you will clearly begin to notice more signs and messages from the angels.

Use this simple mindfulness exercise whenever you can. You can do this exercise anywhere, but I find it most enjoyable to do somewhere with a nice view, such as the beach, a park or anywhere out in nature.

Stop whatever you are doing and begin to look around you. Take a few deep breaths to relax and set the intention to clear your mind of any worries and concerns. Allow yourself to leave behind your day to day life, goals and what needs to be done and just be present in your surroundings. Right now, *this moment*, is all that matters.

One by one, begin going through each of your five senses and notice what is going on around you. Spend a few minutes, or as long as you want, on each of your senses. Fully taking in and being aware of what you are experiencing. It may be helpful to close your eyes for each of the senses other than sight, that way you will have more focus on the individual sense.

Sight:

Look around and notice everything you see, the colors, the textures, all the objects around you. What is moving, what is still? Are some colors brighter and more saturated than others? Look at and notice all the little details you normally don't notice. Allow yourself to be submerged in the visual beauty around you.

Sound:

Listen to the sounds around you. Notice even the subtle sounds you normally tune out. If your inside it may be the lights humming, outside you may hear the rustling of leaves or cars whizzing by. Allow yourself to be immersed in all the subtle and obvious sounds around you. Notice them each, one by one. Then listen to them all at once.

Smell:

What do you smell? It may be flowers or fresh cut grass. Perhaps exhaust or fumes from cars. Inside it may be an air-freshener, laundry or dinner cooking. Smell your hands, your clothes or other items around you. How many smells can you identify around you right now?

Taste:

Focus on your sense of taste. Do you still taste your lunch or morning coffee? Is there a sweet or bitterness inside your mouth? Does the air around you have any taste or is it tasteless? Open and close your mouth, does the taste change?

Touch/Feel:

What do you feel on and around your body? Is the air cool or warm? Do you feel a breeze on your skin or the heat of the sun? Notice how your clothes feel on your body, your feet touching the floor and the pressure of the chair as you sit on it. Can you feel the presence of objects around you even if you can't see them?

INTERNAL SENSATIONS:

Turn your focus inward and notice what you feel inside your body. Notice how it feels to breathe. The air coming in through your nose. Your chest or stomach rising and falling with each breath. Do you have any pain or soreness? Feel your heart beating. Do you feel full or hungry? Notice all the sensations within your body both good and bad.

There is no way to get mindfulness wrong. It is simply about being present in the moment you are in and paying attention to those things we usually forget to notice. Noticing and intentionally paying attention to everything, whether it is good or bad, beautiful or ugly, exciting or boring. Practice being mindful every chance you get, even if it is only for a minute or two. Just like working a muscle, your mindfulness will get stronger with practice.

INCREASE PERIPHERAL AWARENESS

Our eyes can only focus clearly on a small section of what we are looking directly at, but our eyes can see much more than that. What your eyes see beyond what you are directly looking at is blurry and unclear. This area is your peripheral vision. Peripheral awareness is being aware of what is in your peripheral vision. Most of the time our focus is on what we are directly looking at, which results in missing a lot of what is around us. Including signs of angels. You can train your eyes to notice and more clearly see what is in your peripheral vision. Which will allow you to pick up on many more signs and increase your range of awareness.

Practice this exercise to increase your range of peripheral vision, see it more clearly, and become more aware of what is around you in general.

Hold up your two index fingers together in front of your eyes and focus on them. Slowly move your fingers apart but keep looking straight ahead. Continue to slowly move your fingers wide and away from each other until you can just barely see both fingers right at the edge of your range of peripheral vision. As you keep looking straight ahead, focus on your fingers for a few seconds. Wiggle your fingers a little and try to see as much detail in each finger as possible. Then close your eyes and take a break. Repeat the process, starting with your fingers together in front of you and slowly moving them horizontally away from each other three times. Notice how much further you can move your fingers and still see them each time?

Try doing this exercise every day. You will notice the more you practice the further you will be able to move your fingers. You may also notice, after doing this exercise, that the world seems a little brighter and fuller than before. By intentionally using and exercising your peripheral vision, you'll become more aware of and able to see more of what is around you. More of those little details that usually get blurred out and go unnoticed. Now you just need to remember to pay attention to your peripheral vision whenever possible, *especially* when you're looking for signs from the angels.

THE WHAT'S DIFFERENT EXERCISE

For this exercise, you will need a partner to help

you. With your partner sitting across from you, close your eyes and have them change one thing about themselves. When they are done have them tell you to open your eyes. Then try to spot what they changed. Have your partner start off with something obvious like taking off or putting on a jacket and each time change something less and less noticeable. Such as moving their hand from their knee to just a bit higher on their leg.

Take turns with your partner and have fun trying to make it more difficult each time for your partner to notice the difference. Once you get good at spotting the difference on your partner's body have them change things around them and then include the entire room.

This is an excellent and very effective activity to help train your eyes to see details and bits and pieces of everyday life we tend to miss. Angel numbers and other angel signs are often subtle details in the environment that are easy to miss if we are not paying attention and seeing the details. So, use this fun activity as often as possible.

Practice Using All Your Senses

This technique will help you enhance and use all your senses to become aware of what is around you. Just like the other techniques, it is a way for you to become better at picking up on the subtle signs of the angels. This technique is similar to mindfulness. Except you are going to focus only on one sense at a time.

For this activity, you will pick one of your senses

and focus on it intensely while going about your day as usual. Warning… make sure you are not doing something that needs your full attention, you want to be safe while doing this. Try it at home while making dinner or doing chores. Start off with a short amount of time, about 5 minutes. During that time you will intentionally notice and focus on everything coming in through the sense you have chosen.

For example, say you are doing laundry and practicing sight. Do your laundry as usual, but don't tune out as usual. This time focus on fully taking in and noticing everything you see. Pay extra attention to the colors of each garment you wash. Notice the details of the buttons, dials and words on the washer and dryer. See all the details, textures and stitches in the garments you are washing/folding/putting away. Maybe take a minute to watch your washer work or look at how the clothes tumble in the dryer. Look at your hands and how they move and operate while you accomplish each task. Now do this for each of your five senses and for your internal sensations like in the mindfulness practice previously.

The key is just to be more aware of each sense. You're not trying to do anything different than usual or out of the ordinary. You are just practicing being aware of and using each of your senses. Developing each sense, your effectiveness at using them, and increasing your awareness. As you get better at this, increase the time you spend with each sense until you work your way up to doing it for an hour or so.

Learning how to increase your awareness is not only valuable for noticing and receiving signs from the angels. It also helps you to nurture your entire being.

Opening you up to a world and a life that may be passing you by. There is so much more to this existence than just trying to accomplish the expectations we have come to have for ourselves. Putting the time and effort into taking care of yourself and enjoying the life you have makes you more rounded, happier and much more capable of following your spiritual path.

PART TWO
ANGEL NUMBER MESSAGES

How to Use This Guide

Welcome to the guide to angel numbers. In this part of the book, I will take you through the primary angel numbers 1-9 and 0 along with the master numbers 11, 22, and 33. These are the primary angel numbers, and each carries their own unique energy. All other numbers and sequences of numbers are a combination of these thirteen primary numbers. So this guide is all you need to help determine the message of any number or sequence of numbers the angels send your way. You can also find this guide called, *An Easy Guide to Angel Numbers*, on my blog at sarahdawntunis.com/angel-numbers, along with several other number sequences and combinations.

This guide is structured to be easy for you to look up the energy of each angel number and determine what the message is for you. However, it is only a guide. It will help point you in the right direction. But no guide is ever going to completely cover every possible message, so it is up to you to use your skills and knowledge to understand and take your communication with the angels to the next level. The first part of this book includes how to understand the deeper angel number message intended specifically for you, so review that as needed.

Each angel number is divided into three sections. The first section includes keywords related to the energy of that number. Next, you will find a description of the energy that number resonates with and what it means for us in the physical realm. The third and final section includes possible and common messages that occur when seeing that angel number. Once again, keep in mind, these messages are based on a general meaning of the energy of each number and may or may not be all inclusive of what the message intended for you is.

When looking at the messages of each number you may find that one or two of the messages apply to you. Or you may find some combination of all the messages apply to you. Or you may feel that some of it resonates, but you don't feel quite satisfied. As if there is something missing. All these reactions are normal. As you get used to receiving angel number messages and diving deeper into communication with the angels you will find it becomes easier to understand what the angels are intending for you to receive. Give yourself a break, start out slow and always ask the angels when you need help.

Since master numbers work a bit differently than the other numbers, they each have an additional *Challenges* section. This section includes what may be going on in your life when you receive the message, or it could be a warning that if you do not take the advice of the angel number message you may be heading down that road of challenges. Remember master numbers have a more powerful energy, and when that energy is in your life you need to put in the effort to gain mastery of it. By doing so you will experience significant benefits and if you don't, you take the chance of having its negative effects on your life. The blessing or the curse.

As you use and study this guide, keep in mind, all angel numbers mean the angels are with you, guiding you and loving you. Some numbers list this as a message specifically and that means the angels are emphasizing the point. You may also find the meaning and messages of each number seem to overlap or say the same thing. In such cases, be sure to look back through the keywords and energy of the number to help you pick up on the subtle difference of the message. Even similar messages across numbers will differ somewhat when taken in the context of the energy of the number it is associated with.

I know I keep saying this, but please remember, this guide is not all inclusive of every possible message and meaning each angel number carries. Be sure to use your intuition, thoughts, and feelings to guide you toward having and understanding the message the angels intend for you in each individual situation.

With that said, I wish you all the best. <3

ANGEL NUMBER 1
"NEW BEGINNINGS"

KEYWORDS:

- ✓ New Beginnings
- ✓ Fresh Starts
- ✓ Independence
- ✓ Individuality
- ✓ Initiative
- ✓ Instinct
- ✓ Intuition
- ✓ Inspiration
- ✓ Pioneering
- ✓ Uniqueness
- ✓ Potential
- ✓ Opportunity
- ✓ Motivation
- ✓ Ambition
- ✓ Will-power
- ✓ Self-reliance
- ✓ Progress
- ✓ Activity
- ✓ Assertiveness
- ✓ Creation
- ✓ Achievement
- ✓ Success
- ✓ Strength
- ✓ Positivity
- ✓ Interconnectedness
- ✓ Connection to Source

THE ENERGY OF ANGEL NUMBER 1

The angel number 1, often represented by a simple single vertical line, brings the energy of new beginnings and individuality. Just like each of us, as we begin a new journey in life, it stands alone as the first of an infinite amount of numbers and potential to follow. Full of limitless possibilities to become anything.

It represents many of the wonderful aspects of heading into something new and the opportunity to have fresh starts. It is the motivation and inspiration that drive us toward achieving our dreams and goals. It is the action and assertiveness of accomplishing, attaining and creating.

The number one stands for strength and ability. Self-reliance and will-power. It is the positivity and positiveness in life, in us and in what life may bring.

Even though the number one appears to be alone it is anything but lonely. As it represents the unity and connectedness of all things. The idea that all individuals are connected and as one with the Universe, interconnected by energy and created as a piece of the source of all creation.

THE MESSAGE OF ANGEL NUMBER 1

If you have been seeing the angel number 1 repeatedly the message you are receiving from the angels is one of positivity and support. Here is what the angels are telling you.

THE START OF SOMETHING NEW

You may see the angel number 1 as you begin a new phase of your life, enter a new life-changing project or are about to embark on a new journey. The message may appear to you after a major loss when you need to adapt and change in order to adjust to what is now missing in your life. In this case, the angels are letting you know that they support what you are doing and are standing by ready to assist you in the process.

When seeing the angel number 1, you may not yet be aware of the change that is in preparation for your life. In this case, you have angels presenting opportunities for you (perhaps in answer to a prayer or request for help) and they are letting you know to be on the lookout for these possibilities. Open yourself up to the idea of new beginnings and look for where they are manifesting in your life.

Create Something Amazing

Seeing the angel number 1 means it is a wonderful time to create something new and amazing. The angels are supporting and encouraging you to come up with new ideas and strive to turn them into reality. If you are considering starting a project this is your push to get started without delay. The angels are letting you know this is the right thing to do and you have what it takes.

Use your inner-drive, determination, instincts and intuition to accomplish new goals and desires. The angel number 1 carries the energy of success and the motivation to accomplish it. Keep going and don't give up. This is the beginning of something truly wonderful.

Stay Positive

Staying in a positive state of mind can be quite challenging for many of us. But if you have the one energy in your life you really need to do whatever you can to keep your thoughts, actions and emotions as positive as possible. This is a time when things are manifesting very quickly. Whatever you are thinking about you are more likely to attract to you and it will happen much faster than usual.

Especially remember to stay positive on dates that have a lot of ones, such as 1/11 and 11/11. These days carry the one energy for everyone and make it especially strong. So, your thoughts will manifest extremely quickly. Keep them positive and enjoy the benefits.

You Are Not Alone

You may feel fear, uncertainty or doubt, especially when at the beginning of something new. Or you may experience persistent challenges as you work to manifest and achieve your goals. So the angels will send the angel number 1, as a message of reassurance. To let you know they are supporting you. They want you to keep going but know you are not alone. No matter what - the angels have your back.

Take Risks

When you see the angel number 1, the angels are asking you to be willing to step out beyond the zone you feel comfortable in. Often the best changes in life are those that began while taking a risk. Don't miss out on opportunities for something great because you were afraid to leave your safe zone.

Take some chances, try something new and be open to the possibilities. When you do, you open the portal of massive potential where the angels can create miracles and guide you toward greatness.

YOU ARE A CO-CREATOR

The angel number 1 is a reminder that you are a co-creator of your life. You are not a passive observer just waiting for what is going to happen next. You can choose what you want in life and what direction you want to go. Learn about and use the Law of Attraction along with asking the angels for guidance to become the person you want to be and create a life that brings you joy, health and abundance.

The angels want you to know that you are not meant to suffer, rather your physical life is meant to create change and help the world become a better place. When you are in a place of health, happiness and abundance you are in a much better position to assist others and fulfill the purpose God created you for.

ANGEL NUMBER 2
"KEEP THE FAITH"

KEYWORDS:

- ✓ Balance
- ✓ Harmony
- ✓ Faith
- ✓ Trust
- ✓ Service
- ✓ Adaptability
- ✓ Diplomacy
- ✓ Duty to others
- ✓ Cooperation
- ✓ Consideration
- ✓ Compassion
- ✓ Receptivity
- ✓ Relationships
- ✓ Partnerships
- ✓ Divinity
- ✓ Life purpose
- ✓ Peace
- ✓ Inner-peace
- ✓ Love
- ✓ Empathy
- ✓ Insight
- ✓ Intuition
- ✓ The soul's mission

THE ENERGY OF ANGEL NUMBER 2

The angel number 2 has a powerful and majestic energy of faith, diplomacy, balance, harmony and love. Its energy reminds us to create balance and harmony in all our relationships and in every aspect of our lives. To treat others with love, compassion and consideration and in turn, treat ourselves with the same love and respect. Its energy is of our duty to serve not only others but ourselves as well.

Angel number 2 primarily means *"Keep the Faith,"* but this energy is not limited to spiritual faith. It does have the energy of having faith in God, the angels and our spiritual guides despite what we may see and understand through our physical senses. Yet it also carries the energy of having faith and trust in yourself and in your ability to fulfill your divine life purpose. Having faith in who you are and what you can accomplish is synergistic with having faith in the one who created you.

As such, it also carries the energy of intuition and insight. The angel number 2 urges you to trust in what you feel rather than what your five senses are telling you. Since you cannot know what lies just ahead of you, the angel number 2 represents the faith it takes to keep going even in times of doubt.

The angel number 2 has the energy of both love and receptivity. Along with the energy of relationships and partnerships of all kinds - including family, friendships, romantic, business, and ourselves. Bringing the energy of adaptability, diplomacy, cooperation and consideration the angel number 2 represents our ability to create this balance and harmony in all our interactions with others.

Its energy of service and duty encourages serving ourselves by following our life path while also serving the greater good. We create more balance and love in our own lives by serving and reaching out to others.

But we cannot just give and serve others we need to be open and receptive to receiving love and assistance as well. It is just as important to receive as it is to give.

Finally, the angel number 2 brings the energy of peace including inner-peace. By creating balance, having faith and trust, being open to receiving, serving others and pursuing our life purpose we are sure to find our own inner-peace, assist others to find inner-peace and contribute to the creation of a peaceful world.

THE MESSAGE OF ANGEL NUMBER 2

If you have been seeing the angel number 2 repeatedly the message you are receiving from the angels is of reassurance. Here is what the angels are telling you.

FIND AND PURSUE YOUR LIFE PURPOSE

Your divine life purpose, also known as your life path, is what you are meant to accomplish while incarnated in this physical life on earth. When you are energetically aligned with your life purpose you feel a sense of peace, balance and joy. When you are out of alignment feelings of frustration, anxiety, despair and depression will surface.

By seeing the angel number 2, the angels are encouraging you to find your life purpose. Then pursue it with all your heart and soul. Sometimes the world will tell you that you are meant to be doing something different and that may throw you off course. So be sure to go forward with faith. Trust in the angels, yourself, your intuition and your abilities. You have spiritual and universal energies on your side.

Follow your internal guidance and be open to

receiving assistance from the angels so you can find and accomplish your divine life purpose with unwavering faith. You know you are on the right path and aligned with the spiritual when you feel good about what you are doing.

Keep Going

You may be following your life path and putting in a lot of hard work. Yet, our limited physical sight makes it difficult to see that we are going in the right direction and making a difference.

The angels who are sending the angel number 2 can see beyond what you can, and they are letting you know your hard work is, in fact, paying off. Regardless of whether you can see it yet or not - you are getting close - keep going.

Your Prayers are Being Answered

The angel number 2 may appear when you have been praying for something but have not yet received an answer. Once again, the angels are sending a message about what they can see that you cannot. Your prayers are in the process of being answered.

The angels are asking you to have faith and trust. What you have asked for will manifest when it is meant to. The message of angel number 2 is a reminder that our prayers are always heard and answered according to our greater good, but the when and how it is answered is not up to us. Have patience, faith and trust that when it is meant to happen it will.

CREATE HARMONY WITH OTHERS

By sending angel number 2, the angels are encouraging you to create harmony in your relationships and in all your interactions with others. Use diplomacy, cooperation, consideration and love when dealing with others.

This includes your personal relationships and in your service to others. Use empathy and compassion as you interact with people. In relationships, there are always two sides. So put yourself in the other person's point of view to gain a better understanding of what they are going through.

When you see the angel number 2 it is a good time to improve and repair any of your relationships that may be experiencing trouble. But don't stop there, make sure there is balance and harmony in all your relationships. Including the relationship you have with yourself.

CREATE BALANCE

The angel number 2 is a message to create inner-peace and balance within yourself. Be sure you are taking care of yourself physically, mentally and emotionally. Allow time every day to work on and accomplish your dreams and goals.

The message of the angel number 2 is a reminder to open yourself up to opportunities and possibilities by allowing yourself to receive. So many of us know how to give but have never been taught that it is ok to receive. All this serves to do is throw us off balance and make it much harder to accomplish our life purpose.

Ask for help from the angels and open yourself up to receiving their love, guidance and support. Always allow others to give to you and be sure to take care of yourself *as well as* others.

Angel Number 3
"On the Right Path"

Keywords:

- ✓ Optimism
- ✓ Joy
- ✓ Enthusiasm
- ✓ Creativity
- ✓ Imagination
- ✓ Artistic
- ✓ Manifestation
- ✓ Inspiration
- ✓ Youthful
- ✓ Adventure
- ✓ Spontaneity
- ✓ Growth
- ✓ Expansion
- ✓ Increase
- ✓ Abundance
- ✓ Humor
- ✓ Self-expression
- ✓ Inner-wisdom
- ✓ Communication
- ✓ Social connections
- ✓ The Third Eye
- ✓ Ascended Masters
- ✓ The Holy Trinity

The Energy of Angel Number 3

The angel number 3 is the embodiment of living life and walking along our spiritual path with childlike joy, imagination and optimism. It also brings a very spiritual, loving, supportive and protective energy. It is the energy of living life with enthusiasm, forging ahead into the realm of imagination, creativity and adventure without fear. Knowing without a doubt that we are protected and loved by unseen spiritual powers.

The youthful and fun energy of the angel number 3 resonates with strong connections to the spiritual realm and the Universe. Representing the ascended masters, the Holy Trinity and the third eye, the angel number 3 is the energy of spiritual forces being intertwined with our physical lives. Unlike the angel number 2, which reminds us to *keep the faith*, the angel number 3 is the energy of those who already have abundant faith and are living life according to their spiritual calling.

Angel number 3 is the energy of strong spiritual connectedness. Offering us the protection and freedom to live according to our soul's mission. In addition, this strong spiritual connection allows our guardians to hear us clearly and easily answer our prayers. As such, the number three is often seen after praying or when using positive affirmations. It is a sign that your prayer has been heard and is being answered.

The angel number 3 also has the energy of oneness and connection with the Universe and universal energies. Therefore, it also resonates strongly with the energy of imagination and manifestation. Additionally, the energy of abundance, expansion, increase and growth are synonymous with the angel number 3. You can make your dreams come true.

We are not just manifestors, we are co-creators and do best when focusing on the positive aspects of ourselves and life. The angel number 3 carries the energy of humor, optimism and enthusiasm reminding us to live every day with joy and positivity.

The combined energies of the angel number 3 remind us that our external life reflects what is going on inside of us. In other words, you attract into your life what you are feeling and thinking about. So live with love and joy.

Angel number 3 is the energy of self-expression, communication and creativity. As such, it encourages us to think outside the box, try new hobbies or activities and use our artistic and creative abilities as we follow our life path, interact with others and manifest our desires.

The angel number 3 also has the energy of adventure, spontaneity and inspiration. Which clearly guides us toward trusting in ourselves and our abilities. It encourages us to be willing to take risks and step out beyond our comfort zone by trusting in ourselves and the deep connection we have with spiritual and universal energies.

The Message of Angel Number 3

If you have been seeing the angel number 3 repeatedly the message you are receiving from the angels is one of assurance and encouragement. Here is what the angels are telling you.

You Are On the Right Path

There is no doubt when you repeatedly see the angel number 3 you are on the right path. The angels are letting you know they recognize you are truly living a spiritual life. Which means you are on the path of spiritual growth. Because of this, your connection to them is strong. They want you to know they can hear you clearly and are working on answering your prayers. Keep doing what you are doing as this is a message of recognition, reassurance and approval.

Ascended Masters are Helping You

The angel number 3 carries the message of being assisted and watched over by the ascended masters. Ascended masters help us to manifest desires, find peace, understanding and love. They also help us see ourselves and others through the eyes of God.

Your assistance may be coming from any ascended master you feel a strong connection with. Including Jesus, Buddha, Quan Yin, a saint or any spiritual or religious figure. If you see the angel number 3 often, it means you have a very close connection to this ascended master. The angel number 3 is a message from this ascended master letting you know they are here and are helping you. You have their divine love, guidance, help and protection.

You Are Protected

The angels and ascended masters will send the angel number 3 to let you know they are protecting you. You have come to a point along your spiritual journey where they can easily connect with and assist in your day to day life. They are encouraging you to continue along your path without delay or fear because they are protecting you from harm with each step you take.

Take Action

Believe in yourself, take an adventure and be

spontaneous. Follow your intuition and trust your inner guidance. You are encouraged to go with your intuition and follow your heart without hesitation or delay. With such strong spiritual protection, you really cannot go wrong. The angels and ascended masters are encouraging you to realize the deepness and power of your spiritual connection. By doing so you can live according to your life path and accomplish your dreams.

TAKE CHANCES

By seeing the angel number 3, the angels are encouraging you to take chances. Since you have so much protection and support, now is the time to put yourself out there and take some risks. Do what you have been putting off out of anxiety or fear. The angel number 3 means you are on a path of spiritual growth, and you are being encouraged to get out there and try new things that will help further your growth, live according to your life path and to manifest your desires.

LIVE YOUR LIFE WITH LOVE, JOY AND OPTIMISM

The angels are letting you know that your connection to universal energy is strong. As such your ability to manifest your desires is also strong. They remind you to live your life and follow your life path with love, joy and optimism. Trust in your abilities, skills and talents as they will help you to manifest the life you deserve to have. Try not to doubt yourself. Remember you have the support and approval of spiritual and universal energies right now. Your prayers and positive affirmations are being heard. So, go and live with enthusiasm for what the future will bring.

Be Creative and Artistic

Use your creative skills and abilities. If you have been working on a creative or artistic project, the angels are encouraging you to share it with the world. Or they might be encouraging you to follow a creative or artistic project you have been thinking about recently.

The angels also encourage you to use your creativity and artistic abilities to manifest your desires, follow your life path and to assist others. If you have been thinking about writing a book, painting, sculpture, dancing or any other creative endeavor, now is the time to do it and share it with the world. The angels are letting you know this is the path to not only enhancing your own life but also the lives of others.

ANGEL NUMBER 4
"TIME TO FOCUS"

KEYWORDS:

- ✓ Organization
- ✓ Devotion
- ✓ Application
- ✓ Trust
- ✓ Dignity
- ✓ Endurance
- ✓ Loyalty
- ✓ Mastery
- ✓ Solid foundations
- ✓ Determination
- ✓ Production
- ✓ Hard-work
- ✓ Morals
- ✓ Values
- ✓ Honesty
- ✓ Integrity
- ✓ Conscientiousness
- ✓ Dependability
- ✓ Conviction
- ✓ Security
- ✓ Self-control
- ✓ Reality
- ✓ Stability
- ✓ Progress
- ✓ Management
- ✓ Justice
- ✓ Discipline
- ✓ Order
- ✓ The Archangels
- ✓ The Four Elements (Earth, Air, Wind & Fire)
- ✓ The Four Sacred Directions (North, South, East & West

The Energy of Angel Number 4

The angel number 4 brings a down-to-earth practical energy. It is the energy of building strong foundations and creating safety, security and stability as a basis for accomplishing our dreams, desires and soul's purpose. While many of the numbers encourage us to dream and reach for the stars, the angel number 4 is the practicality and reality of how to accomplish those dreams.

With the energy of devotion, loyalty, mastery, determination, and self-control, the angel number 4 resonates with the energy of our desire to get down to business and achieve whatever it is we set our minds to. It is the side of us that decides what is important and has the passion and dedication to get it done. It is the energy of being grounded, determined and focused.

Angel number 4 represents how to accomplish our goals while on the physical plane. So, it carries the energy of organization, management, system and order, application, production, hard work, ability, progress, seriousness, discipline, dependability and conviction. All of which reminds us that living on the physical plane requires us to make plans and put in the work required to achieve our goals. Goals large and small benefit from the implementation of the energies of the angel number 4.

The angel number 4 represents our ability to accomplish anything but it is best done with the greater good of all in mind. This is because its energy resonates with accomplishing our dreams and living our lives with integrity, pragmatism, dignity, trustworthiness, honesty, high morals, values, conscientiousness and justice.

The angel number 4 resonates highly with the archangels. The archangels are known to manage and organize the realm of angels and make sure all runs smoothly. The archangels are masters of the angel number 4's energy. The angel number 4 also carries the energy of the archangels being around us - available to call on at any time. They are our connection of the physical plane to the spiritual plane.

Finally, the earthly energies of the angel number 4 resonate with the four elements of Earth, Air, Wind and Fire. And with the four sacred directions North, South, East and West.

The Message of Angel Number 4

If you have been seeing the angel number 4 repeatedly the message you are receiving from the angels is of assistance. Here is what the angels are telling you.

You are Surrounded by Angels

By seeing the angel number 4 you are receiving the message that angels, particularly the archangels, are surrounding you. They are supporting you and willing to help you in life and as you accomplish your goals. Remember you have free will and the angels will not interfere in your life without your permission. So ask them for their assistance. By doing so you allow them to create miracles and assist you in accomplishing your goals, dreams and life purpose.

Take Care of Your Physical Needs

The earthly energy of angel number 4 is a reminder to take care of your physical body and the physical space around you. Make sure you are grounded. Take care of your health and body by eating well and getting sufficient exercise.

When you see the angel number 4 it is a good time to implement organization and planning into your physical surroundings. Try cleaning out your closets and getting rid of anything that you no longer need or use. Learn the art of Feng Shui to create strong positive energy in your home and surroundings.

Create Safety and Stability

Whenever you see the angel number 4 make sure you are feeling a sense of safety and stability in all areas of your life. While incarnated in this physical life it is necessary to feel safe and secure before you can effectively accomplish anything else. Having a sense of safety in our physical, emotional, career and relationships allows us to focus on bigger more lofty goals. Do what it takes to create stability all around you. This is the foundation you will build upon, so it needs to be strong.

Make Your Dreams Reality

The angels are encouraging you to turn your dreams into reality. Perhaps you have a goal in mind or you have been procrastinating and looking for the perfect moment to start. This is your message that *now* is the time to start. You have a lot of angels supporting you and urging you to take steps to accomplish your dreams. So now is as good a time as ever to sit down and start figuring out how to make your dreams reality.

It is Time to Focus

As you work on your goals, the angel number 4 is a message that you need to take a step back and really focus on what you are trying to accomplish. Whether you are starting a new goal or already in the midst of it, the angels are urging you to have good organization and lots of preparation in place.

Create a strong foundation and build security and stability into your plans through a healthy dose of organization and planning. Break down big goals into small accomplishable steps. Rely on practicality and logic. This is a common message for those of us who tend to have high, lofty goals but trouble accomplishing it all.

Challenge Yourself

The angels are encouraging you to challenge yourself as you work to accomplish your goals. This means if you are trying to make a decision - choose the more challenging road. The angel number 4 has the energy of conviction, determination, passion and drive. So now is a great time to put those skills to use. Challenge yourself to accomplish things you may normally shy away from. You may find that you are up to the challenge.

ANGEL NUMBER 5
"ON WINGS OF CHANGE"

KEYWORDS:

- ✓ Transformation
- ✓ Change
- ✓ Freedom (personal)
- ✓ Individuality
- ✓ Companionability
- ✓ Life lessons
- ✓ Choices
- ✓ Decisions
- ✓ Intelligence
- ✓ Variety
- ✓ Adaptability
- ✓ Versatility
- ✓ Non-attachment
- ✓ Motivation
- ✓ Progress
- ✓ Activity
- ✓ Travel
- ✓ Adventure
- ✓ Sympathy
- ✓ Understanding
- ✓ Release
- ✓ Surrender
- ✓ Influence
- ✓ Promotion
- ✓ Courage
- ✓ Curiosity
- ✓ Idealism
- ✓ Health
- ✓ Vision
- ✓ Expansion
- ✓ Opportunity
- ✓ Mercy
- ✓ Kindness
- ✓ Invention
- ✓ Competitiveness
- ✓ The heart (proverbial)

The Energy of Angel Number 5

The angel number 5 brings the energy of positive and significant change. Yet, it is not the energy of ordinary change. Rather it signifies a divine metamorphosis of past experiences merging together to create something new and different.

A change that is much like the transformation of the butterfly. In fact, the caterpillar will outgrow and shed its skin four times. It is the 5th time of going through this cycle it will instead hang from a branch to form a chrysalis. From which it will emerge a butterfly.

The angel number 5 resonates with the energy of such positive, necessary and life-long change.

It also resonates with the energy of personal freedom and individuality. Representing our ability to free ourselves from the past allowing ourselves to grow and adapt physically, mentally and spiritually.

Carrying the energy of versatility, adaptability, non-attachment, variety and release/surrender the angel number 5 reminds us to learn and grow from our past experiences, but also be willing to let them go so we are not ruled by them.

Like the caterpillar who must summon the courage to venture into vast and unknown change, the angel number 5 represents the courage it takes for us to not only make positive life choices but also the resourcefulness and motivation to take on the activity and the adventure of making these changes a reality.

The angel number 5 also resonates with the proverbial heart. Sending us the reminder that because you are the only one to know your true heart's desire you are the only one who can follow your true passions and achieve your destiny.

Although the angel number 5 represents the kind of change we ultimately go through alone, at the same time it resonates with the energy of companionability, mercy and kindness. Reminding us that our relationships with others are a significant part of our individual life and success. This also brings the energy of being surrounded by angels and spiritual guides.

The Message of Angel Number 5

If you have been seeing the angel number 5 repeatedly the message you are receiving from the angels is one of preparation and support. Here is what the angels are telling you.

Change is Occurring

By seeing the angel number 5 the angels are sending a message that a major and positive change is in your near future. In fact, this change has probably been in the process of occurring for a while now. Perhaps for weeks, months or even years.

When the caterpillar enters the chrysalis, the wings it will have as a butterfly have already begun to grow - unseen beneath the surface. You also are about to emerge through a major life change, but the transformation has already begun.

Be Prepared

The angels want you to keep a grateful and positive

state of mind. This will allow you to be in a place to accept and adapt to the change as it occurs. They understand, for many of us, change is hard and venturing into the unknown is scary. So they are sending you this message to prepare you.

The angels want you to understand that this change will take courage, but it is good. It will bring benefits to you for the rest of your life. By keeping a positive outlook and an open mind you allow the change you are about to go through to be the positive life-long change you are meant to receive.

Angels are Surrounding You

Whether this change is wanted or scary. Expected or out of the blue. No matter what kind of transformation your life may be going through, the angels want you to know they are surrounding you and ready to assist you. Remember to call on them for help if this change ever feels daunting or scary.

Be Kind To Yourself

The angels urge you to treat yourself with kindness and mercy. During times of change, it is easy to get caught up in judgment and negativity of ourselves. The angels remind you to look at yourself through their eyes and through the eyes of those who love you. Remember to implement a lot of self-care all the time but especially as you go through this change.

Free Yourself

In order to grow and have the full benefits of the change that is upon you, you'll need to free yourself from the restraints of your past. Now is the time to let go of your past. Taking with you the lessons from your experiences and releasing anything that holds you back.

"Out with the old, in with the new," is a good phrase to keep in mind.

Once the butterfly is born, its lifestyle will become completely different than it was before its wings emerged. Unlike the caterpillar, it will enjoy the freedom of flight and the sweetness of nectar, but its purpose will also be different. To try to continue living as a caterpillar would deny the butterfly of its destiny.

Follow Your Heart

The change occurring in your life is positive and divinely guided. Although such a big change may seem overwhelming it is for your greater good. It will be worth it.

To gain the full benefit of this change, you need to take action. You have earned this change, but it will not happen if you do not act upon the opportunity before you.

So, the angel number 5 is a message to follow your heart. Avoid listening to the ego or any negative or self-defeating talk. The angels are sending you this message, so your actions do not end up getting in the way. Follow your heart, including your passions, imagination and desires and you will be able to assist this divine change without allowing any fear of change to stand in the way.

Take A Break

The primary message of angel number 5 is about

change and transformation, however, the angels may also send this number as a message to take a break. Your mind has been heavily focused on many things and the angels are supportive of your efforts. But they are saying you need to step back and take some time to heal and grow through rest and relaxation. Take a vacation or go somewhere new to gain a different perspective. This is an excellent time to travel (physically or even just in your mind) and learn something new.

"What the caterpillar calls the end of the world the master calls a butterfly."
- Richard Bach

ANGEL NUMBER 6
"TOO MUCH WORRY"

KEYWORDS:

- ✓ Balance
- ✓ Harmony
- ✓ Peace
- ✓ Stability
- ✓ Unconditional love
- ✓ Home
- ✓ Family
- ✓ Parenthood
- ✓ Domesticity
- ✓ Guardianship
- ✓ Service
- ✓ Selflessness
- ✓ Responsibility
- ✓ Self-sacrifice
- ✓ Nurturing
- ✓ Care
- ✓ Empathy
- ✓ Sympathy
- ✓ Emotional depth
- ✓ Adjustment
- ✓ Stability
- ✓ Protection
- ✓ Firmness
- ✓ Justice
- ✓ Conscientiousness
- ✓ Teaching
- ✓ Problem-solving
- ✓ Seeing clearly
- ✓ Conviction
- ✓ Curiosity
- ✓ Grace
- ✓ Dignity
- ✓ Simplicity
- ✓ Reliability
- ✓ Material needs
- ✓ Economy
- ✓ Agriculture
- ✓ Growth

The Energy of Angel Number 6

The angel number 6 is the most domestic of all the numbers. A domestic energy of our family and our connection to the entire planet. It can be summed up as the energy of Mother Nature. A loving, nurturing energy that protects and provides for all the earth and its inhabitants. It is an energy of balance, harmony and unconditional love.

The energy of the angel number 6 resonates highly with many of our material and physical needs. It also resonates with our deepest emotions. People often see the angel number 6 when living life unbalanced and too focused on the material world.

The angel number 6 has a very earthly energy as it represents agriculture, material needs, economy, and growth. It has the energy of what we need to live in the material world. However, its earthly energy is about more than just physical and financial needs. As it also brings the energy of peace, honesty, integrity, healing, justice, conscientiousness and humanitarianism. Everything on the earth is part of our greater family and needs to be treated as such.

With the energy of home and family, parenthood, guardianship, emotional depth and unconditional love it represents the domestic side of life. The need to take care of others and the ever-important role of taking care of our home and family. It also has the energy of self-sacrifice, selflessness, empathy, sympathy, nurturing, care and service to others. All of which are reminders that there is more to life than accomplishing goals and financially supporting those we love. Like

Mother Nature, we are here to support the earth and all its inhabitants.

The angel number 6 brings the energy of stability. It represents our need for balance in life and our ability to create stability through problem-solving, seeing clearly, curiosity, grace and dignity. Like the role of parents and caregivers, it also represents our ability to teach others how to have such stability in their lives.

THE MESSAGE OF ANGEL NUMBER 6

If you have been seeing the angel number 6 repeatedly the message you are receiving from the angels is one of loving advice. Here is what the angels are telling you.

CHANGE YOUR FOCUS

By seeing the angel number 6 you are being told that your focus has been on the wrong things. Perhaps you have been worrying a lot about money, having negative thoughts, or spending too much time and energy at work. As a result, you are attracting more worry and more of what you are worried about to yourself. You are being called to take a step back and shift your focus to positive things.

The angels urge you to focus on all things positive and let go of the negative. Change your focus to what you are grateful for rather than what you lack. To spending time with your family rather than spending so much time working. To having faith and trust rather than worry and fear.

The message of the angel number 6 is that your earthly and material needs are being taken care of - ***you do not need to worry so much.***

Create Stability with Balance

Your physical and earthly needs are important for your life on earth. Money helps create security and stability. However, the angels are sending you the angel number 6 because you are lacking the stability you are working so hard for. This is due to a lack of balance in your life and not a lack of material needs.

The angels are letting you know that you have been worrying too much about the material world. By doing so you have been neglecting your spiritual side. This worry is creating blocks and the angels are not able to send their assistance. You need to let your worries go and have faith that your physical needs are being taken care of. Nurture your spiritual side with faith, love and expectation.

Create balance by having faith and by being open to the opportunities for financial and physical abundance that *will* present themselves. Be sure to balance work with play, your spiritual side with your physical side, and your worries with plenty of positive thinking and gratitude.

Help Others

The angel number 6 is calling you to reach out and help others. If you have been focused a lot on your own material needs and worries, now is a good time to reach out and help those who need help more than you. It serves as a reminder of how much you have, encouraging an attitude of gratitude. Remember to treat those you help as kindly and lovingly as you would a member of your family.

By nurturing, caring for and serving those in need

you are fulfilling your life purpose and serving the greater good. Not to mention it will shift your attraction from lack to abundance. As the energy you put out by giving is that you have enough to give. And who doesn't want to attract "enough" into their lives? Especially if it can be done while helping others at the same time.

Family and Domestic Matters

Those who are part of your family are not always biologically or legally defined. Family (especially in the sense of the angel number 6) is what you feel in your heart - therefore anyone can be family. With that said, the angel number 6 may be calling your attention to your family. Here are a few possibilities:

Someone Needs You

Perhaps someone in your family needs you. Your natural empathy and nurturing are heightened right now so you can be there to help those who will benefit from your domestic abilities. You are being called to pay attention to those you love because someone may need your help, love and empathy now or in the near future.

A Change is Coming

The angel number 6 may be calling your attention to a change that is about to occur that will affect your family. This change may be something like a move, an addition to your family or a death. The angels want you to know that this change is good, and they are supporting you. Call on them whenever you need help staying positive during this change.

Family Is Part of Your Life Path

When seeing the angel number 6 you may be receiving the message that having a family of your own is part of your life path. If you are already married and/or have children, the message you are receiving is supporting the path you are on.

If you are single the angel number 6 may be letting you know to be open to marriage and children as it is in your future and meant to be. Keep an eye out for a soul mate who may show up very soon.

It may also mean you are meant to work with children and/or families. Or the message may be calling you to adopt or do foster care.

Follow your heart and be open to possibilities and your life path will become clear. You can also call on the angels for support or clarification in understanding what your life path is.

ANGEL NUMBER 7
"KEEP IT UP"

KEYWORDS:

- Spirituality
- All things spiritual
- Religion
- The esoteric
- The metaphysical
- The mind
- All sciences
- Education
- Teaching
- Writers
- The written word
- Healers
- Healing
- Luck & Good Fortune
- Our internal world
- Inner-selves
- Emotions
- Thoughts
- Virtue
- Dignity
- Compassion
- Unrestricted
- Non-conformity
- Independence
- Thinking outside the box
- Drive
- Determination
- Purpose
- Passion
- Evolvement
- Completion
- Perfectionism
- Silence
- Inner-strength
- Endurance
- Intention

- ✓ Intuition
- ✓ Introspection
- ✓ Contemplation
- ✓ Secrets
- ✓ Myths
- ✓ Peace
- ✓ Manifestation
- ✓ Meditation
- ✓ The Collective Consciousness

The Energy of Angel Number 7

The angel number 7 is a very spiritual number that resonates deeply with our mind and internal world. It is the energy of all things to do with what we think, feel and understand. It is the world that lies within each of us as individuals that is ultimately untouchable by anyone else. This is where the physical-self meets and combines with the spiritual-self. Within is where it all comes together and becomes one. The angel number 7 is the embodiment of the connection between physical and spiritual.

The energy of the angel number 7 is solitary and independent. It is a personal energy that lies deep within us. Yet once we have an awareness of this deep internal world of isolation we find it is where all things physical and spiritual connect and merge together as one. All things as one connected by the almighty force of creation. Known as the collective consciousness, we are all connected and are part of the divine.

The angel number 7 brings the energy of accomplishment, especially regarding spirituality. By seeing this number, you know you are making the right decisions and headed in the right direction.

It carries the energy of doing what is needed to accomplish your divine life purpose. It is the energy of persistence and perseverance and overcoming obstacles and hardships with grace, dignity and by listening to your own inner-wisdom.

The angel number 7 resonates with all things spiritual. Including faith and spiritual awareness, awakening, development, acceptance, and enlightenment. Resonating with the Collective Conscious, mysticism, religion and psychic abilities, the angel number 7 carries the energy of all spiritual concepts and practices.

The search for knowledge is a significant energy for the angel number 7 and it resonates with education, learning, writing, study and understanding. It also carries the energy of understanding our physical world through science, technology and logic.

The angel number 7 is a reminder that as we work to further develop ourselves mentally, spiritually and emotionally we can and will accomplish our divine life purpose. That we instinctively have what it takes to know, understand and implement what is needed to fulfill our purpose.

THE MESSAGE OF ANGEL NUMBER 7

If you have been seeing the angel number 7 repeatedly the message you are receiving from the angels is one of celebration. Here is what the angels are telling you.

KEEP DOING WHAT YOU ARE DOING

By seeing the angel number 7, the angels are saying you have been successful in working toward your spiritual development and life purpose. They are letting you know they are very approving of the decisions and choices you have made. You are at a place where you have overcome obstacles and hardships by listening to your divine inner-guidance. The benefits of this success will allow good and positive things to flow freely into your life. You are certainly on the right path, keep doing what you are doing.

Lucky You

The choices, decisions and plans you have made in your life have put you in a place where positive divine energy is able to reach you easily and frequently. The Angels can send their assistance to help you along your path with ease. The angel number 7 reminds you to be open and aware of the opportunities that will present themselves to you. Listen to your intuition and inner-wisdom because they will continue to guide you toward everything you need in life.

Pass It On

The angel number 7 is a message that you are meant to assist others. You are being called to serve others through teaching and healing. Your life purpose is likely related to spirituality and heart-centered services. The angels encourage you to pass on your success to others by teaching, guiding and setting an example to inspire all people to find their own love, passions and life purpose. You are a guiding light.

You Are Right

If you are currently making plans or wondering if a certain decision is right for you, the angel number 7 is confirmation that you are on the right path. Whatever you have been feeling in your heart and feel guided to do is the right decision. Go with it.

Trust Yourself

The angels are sending a message to trust yourself. Look inward and listen to your inner-guidance and knowing. Your intuition is strong and will guide you in the direction you are meant to go. The angel number 7 means you really have no reason to doubt yourself nor your instincts. Listen to your thoughts and feelings as this is how the angels will often communicate with you.

Your Connection Is Strong

When you see the angel number 7 you may be receiving a message that you are reaching a higher level of spiritual awareness and enlightenment. You may experience things that seem unexplainable or out of the ordinary. The world around you may look and feel differently. At this time, you may see signs from the angels more frequently and your understanding of their messages may be clearer and more intense. You may also begin to experience a psychic awareness and a development or increase in psychic abilities.

The angels are letting you know that, although some of these experiences and changes within you may feel strange and uncomfortable at first, this is happening due to the work you have put in to become more connected and aware of the spiritual. Your work toward achieving your life path has now resulted in your being more in-tune to the world most people are completely unaware of. The angels are with you and assisting you through this time. Soon you will get used to these new perceptions and experiences and everything will settle and fall into place.

ANGEL NUMBER 8
"INFINITE POTENTIAL"

KEYWORDS:

- ✓ Potential
- ✓ Prosperity
- ✓ Abundance
- ✓ Money
- ✓ Material Freedom
- ✓ Finances
- ✓ Riches
- ✓ Success
- ✓ Ability
- ✓ Achievement
- ✓ Ambition
- ✓ Decisiveness
- ✓ Divine purpose
- ✓ Authority
- ✓ Challenge
- ✓ Insight
- ✓ Caution
- ✓ Planning
- ✓ Reward
- ✓ Infinity
- ✓ Connectedness
- ✓ Balance
- ✓ Fairness
- ✓ Wholeness
- ✓ Cycles
- ✓ Effort
- ✓ Management
- ✓ Confidence
- ✓ Empowerment
- ✓ Higher energies
- ✓ Lower energies
- ✓ The Ego
- ✓ Dictatorship
- ✓ Discrimination
- ✓ Authoritarianism
- ✓ Control
- ✓ The Law of Cause & Effect

- ✓ Karma
- ✓ Humanity

The Energy of the Angel Number 8

The angel number 8, written as a single stroke looping around to end where it first began, represents infinity and connectedness.

Within the single stroke of the number 8, exists two separate loops, each representing the balance of both higher and lower energies within us and within our physical lives. It is the combination of both higher energy and lower energy that creates the whole.

The angel number 8 reminds us that even though life has its down times, by hanging in there and having faith it always returns to the beginning or top. Creating a whole and complete cycle. Our growth in this life is dependent on all our experiences, good, bad, easy and difficult, coming together as a whole.

If you turn the number 8 onto its side it becomes the sign of infinity. The loops are no longer one above the other, rather they reside on an even level. Reminding us that the ups and downs in life are equal in value and importance.

The angel number 8 brings the energy of putting in the effort and receiving abundance and reward as a result. Without the effort, the reward is not possible.

The angel number 8 has the energy of money, riches, finances, abundance, prosperity and manifesting wealth. It is the energy of material reward directly related to putting in the work and the effort to achieve prosperity on earth. Since it also has the energy of infinity it reminds us that there is enough money for everyone to live in abundance.

The angel number 8 brings the energy of infinite balance and fairness. It holds the energy of Karma and the Universal Law of Cause and Effect. Both of which state that our thoughts and actions will come back to us. It represents how the work we put into our dreams, goals and self-growth will return with infinite abundance and reward, both in this life and the next.

The angel number 8 resonates strongly with your highest potential while incarnated in this lifetime. It is the energy of finding, focusing on and realizing your potential to bring balance and make the world a better place. Whether you know it or not, your potential is infinite. As you accomplish the phases and cycles of your life you can accomplish and grow even more. Making your potential unending.

Although the angel number 8 brings the positive energy of abundance, balance and reward - **beware** of the lower energies that can result if we get stuck in negativity. The angel number 8 brings the lower energies of the ego, dictatorship and discrimination. Resisting these parts of our human nature or giving into these lower energies will result in an infinite loop of negativity. Which reminds us that keeping our thoughts, feelings and actions positive and in balance is part of being human and a necessary part of living according to our life's path.

THE MESSAGE OF ANGEL NUMBER 8

If you have been seeing the angel number 8 repeatedly the message you are receiving from the angels is one of encouragement reminding you of your infinite potential. Here is what the angels are telling you.

Your Hard Work Is Paying Off

The most common message of the angel number 8 is that you are coming upon significant financial abundance. Yet, this abundance is not due to any kind of good luck or good fortune. It is a direct result of your own effort, diligence, and intelligence in working toward achieving your goals. The angels are letting you know to keep working, having faith and being grateful and positive for what you have achieved because the results are about to literally pay off.

Remember to stay positive though. In order to receive this reward, you have to be open to it. Create a path for abundance to flow into your life by keeping your thoughts and focus positive and on what you desire.

Keep It Up

The angels want you to know that you are on the right path to achieving your dreams and goals. They are encouraging you and reminding you to keep going on your path of progress. Keep working to achieve your goals because you have already set yourself in motion for success and achievement. If you stay on this path rewards will infinitely continue to come.

Be Grateful

By seeing the angel number 8, the angels are reminding you to stay positive, optimistic and grateful. You are on the path of reward and manifesting prosperity. Keeping your energy high with positive thoughts and actions will lead you to financial abundance. Be grateful for what you are about to receive so you can ensure that it will reach you.

Achieve Your Highest Potential

The angels want you to know that your life path is important for the greater good of all. They are encouraging you to live up to your highest potential. They are sending you a message of empowerment. Letting you know you have what it takes to achieve more than you know.

Trust and have faith in your abilities, skills and talents and use them to reach out and give to others. Listen to your intuition and internal guidance as it will lead you in the right direction. Put in the work and effort when necessary to achieve your goals and create a solid foundation for your future. The financial reward and abundance that results by living up to your full potential will allow you to continue along your life path and ultimately make the world a better place.

You're on the Wrong Path

There may be times you'll see the angel number 8 because you are stuck in a cycle of pessimism and negativity. You may be experiencing depression, anxiety or a challenging or difficult time in your life. In this case, the angels are letting you know that you have their full support, encouragement and love.

The angels are encouraging you to change your focus. Your negativity has you stuck, and you are only attracting more negativity into your life. They want to remind you to think positive thoughts, be grateful for what you already have and do what it takes to get out of the negative cycle you are stuck in. Even if you are going through a difficult time, the angels are reminding you to hold positive expectations and intentions for your future and of the potential you hold.

Once you put in the effort to be more positive and optimistic you will find that abundance and reward will be able to flow freely into your life. The angels remind you to ask them for help and put in the work and effort to feel better. Because the life of abundance and prosperity that you deserve is not out of reach.

ANGEL NUMBER 9
"YOUR SOUL'S MISSION"

KEYWORDS:

- ✓ Completion
- ✓ The Soul's Mission
- ✓ Life purpose
- ✓ Destiny
- ✓ Spiritual enlightenment
- ✓ Spiritual awareness
- ✓ Spiritual awakening
- ✓ Spiritual growth
- ✓ Life phases
- ✓ The soul
- ✓ Desires
- ✓ Growth
- ✓ Natural skills & talents
- ✓ The higher-self
- ✓ Intuition
- ✓ Internal guidance
- ✓ Faith
- ✓ Trust
- ✓ Believing in yourself
- ✓ Integrity
- ✓ Strength
- ✓ Compassion
- ✓ Love
- ✓ Selflessness
- ✓ Altruism
- ✓ Service
- ✓ Humanitarianism
- ✓ Philanthropy
- ✓ Lightworkers
- ✓ Giving & Receiving
- ✓ Universal energies
- ✓ Universal laws
- ✓ Seeing ourselves & the world through the eyes of God

The Energy of Angel Number 9

Just as nine is the last of the single-digit numbers, the angel number 9 brings the energy of completion. It reminds us that phases in life come to an end so that we can move on to grow, change and complete the mission of our soul.

With the energy of spiritual enlightenment, awareness and awakening, the angel number 9 is the attainment of our life's purpose and completion of our spiritual growth. Most commonly, it represents the end of each phase of growth as we move on and attain our spiritual mission.

In addition, the angel number 9 represents the soul and its desires to accomplish and walk our life's path. Because of this, it carries the energy of our natural skills and talents enabling us to accomplish the soul's mission. Since we are never really alone, the angel number 9 reminds us to look to our higher-self for guidance, love and understanding. As such, the angel number 9 encourages us to follow our intuition and internal guidance with faith and trust.

It is the ability to believe in yourself despite any adversity or the need for outside confirmation. The knowledge that our natural skills, abilities and talents are in perfect harmony with our purpose. Even when others try to persuade us to change or do something differently, it is the energy of maintaining faith and belief in ourselves and what we are doing.

Angel number 9 is the number of integrity, strength, compassion and love. The highly spiritual and universally connected number carries the energy of lightworkers, being of service to others, humanitarianism and philanthropy. Representing those who have a natural ability to heal, nurture and care for others.

It represents those who see the world through love and compassion and work in service of the greater good with no strings attached. They are the angels of the earth who constantly work to make the world a better place and never care who notices all the good they have done.

The energy of the angel number 9 also represents the ability to rise above our problems and physical limitations to see the world, the people of the world and ourselves from the divine eyes of God. Problems are seen from the perspective of pure love and understanding. Our abilities and talents are seen as wonderous and needed. Service to others and our work on earth is seen without the need for recognition. When the problems of life feel too big to manage, the angel number 9 encourages us to rise above and view whatever stands in our way from the eyes of God, the angels and the higher-self.

Finally, the angel number 9 brings the energy of balance between giving and receiving. It reminds us that receiving is just as important as giving. All of us need to balance our lives between being of service and allowing others to be of service to us. As such, the angel number 9 carries the energy of Universal love, Karma and all spiritual laws. Reminding us that the energy we put out will come back to us. The more good you do the more good you will receive.

The Message of Angel Number 9

If you have been seeing the angel number 9 repeatedly the message you are receiving from the angels is one of encouragement. Here is what the angels are telling you.

The End of a Phase

The angels may be letting you know that you have come to the end of something in your life. It may be the end of a life stage, a relationship or a project that you have been working on. In this case, the angels want you to know that this change is part of your purpose and is for the greater good. This change is due to a completion. You have learned and gotten out of this phase what you need to grow and soon will be ready to move on to the next phase of your life.

This is a time to prepare yourself for what comes next. The angel number 9 is about taking action and following your soul in order to further your spiritual development. So, as this phase of your life ends, a new one will begin and, as such, you will have work to do.

The angels are letting you know that they are supporting you through this change and as you begin the next phase. Because of this, you can call on them for guidance and support in adapting, understanding and managing this change.

Let Go of What No Longer Serves You

The angels are sending you the message to let go of that which no longer serves you. As we go through each cycle or phase of life our needs change. As such, it is necessary to let go of the old so there is plenty of room for the new and better parts of yourself and your life.

The angels encourage you to do some mental, emotional and even environmental housecleaning. Clear yourself of old self-defeating thoughts and feelings. Release unhealthy relationships and patterns. Clear your home of clutter and items you no longer use.

You will find as you release the old you will feel lighter, more joyful and motivated. These feelings will prepare you to take the action needed to further accomplish your life's purpose.

BE OF SERVICE TO OTHERS

The angel number 9 is the number of lightworkers. So being of service may come naturally to you. You are now being called to serve others in an uplifting way. Use your natural talents and abilities to be of service to others. Treat all people you come across with love and compassion regardless of the situation. Also, you may be called to change your career to one in the helping profession. or you could be called to volunteer or contribute to charity in some way. Listen to your intuition and your higher-self to guide you in the right direction of humanitarianism.

A LOVED ONE NEEDS YOU

By seeing the angel number 9 the angels may be alerting you to someone who is in need of your help. Someone you know may need your support and unconditional love at this time to get through a difficult situation. Seek out those you know and love and check in on how they are doing.

Take Action Toward Your Dreams and Life Purpose

The angel number 9 is about taking action and using our natural skills, talents and abilities to accomplish our life purpose and to be of service to others. By seeing the angel number 9 the angels are encouraging you to take action toward your dreams. The soul is driven to accomplish its mission. Dreams are the manifestation of the soul's desires. So, you are being encouraged to follow your dreams as a way to accomplish your soul's mission. This is a message to stop procrastinating and take action now. Put your dreams and desires on the top of your list of priorities and take steps every day to reach your goals.

Your Soul is On A Mission

The angel number 9 is the number of the soul and its desire to accomplish its divine mission while on earth. The angels are urging you to learn to listen to your soul's desires and guidance. Accept yourself for who you are and who you are meant to be. You are the perfect creation to accomplish the mission of your soul. Use your intuition and let love and compassion guide you along your path.

Trust and Rely on Your Higher-Self

The angel number 9 is a reminder to follow your internal guidance system. By listening to your gut and your intuition you are tapping into your higher-self where you can more clearly achieve and accomplish all your dreams and desires. The angels want you to learn to trust yourself and have faith in your ability to serve your purpose and manifest the life you are meant to have.

Do Not Worry What Other People Think

The angels want you to realize what other people think is not important to your mission. You are called to follow your higher-self with integrity, compassion and love. Without fear of judgment. Do not worry what other people think, keep your focus on your desires and your own divine destiny. There is nothing wrong with putting yourself and your spiritual growth first. As a matter of fact, it is necessary for your spiritual development.

Balance Giving with Receiving

Remember that receiving is just as important as giving. If you are seeing the angel number 9 you are likely giving a lot of yourself to others and you may find it easy to forget to take care of yourself and your own needs. Although your work is important and necessary, it is just as important to allow yourself to receive help and to take care of your own needs. Remember to nurture your inner-child and take the time to play, rest and relax whenever you need to. By taking care of yourself you are in a much better position to serve others and accomplish your soul's mission.

ANGEL NUMBER 0
"GOD'S LOVING EMBRACE"

KEYWORDS:

- ✓ Spiritual Journey
- ✓ Spirit
- ✓ Prayer
- ✓ Meditation
- ✓ Source
- ✓ Creation
- ✓ Eternity
- ✓ Infinity
- ✓ Wholeness
- ✓ Oneness
- ✓ Flow
- ✓ Potential
- ✓ Choice
- ✓ Cycles
- ✓ Continuation
- ✓ Authenticity
- ✓ Universal Energies
- ✓ Beginning
- ✓ Completion
- ✓ Everything
- ✓ Nothing
- ✓ The Alpha
- ✓ The Omega
- ✓ God Force

THE ENERGY OF ANGEL NUMBER 0

Imagine the energy of God reaching down to you. Arms of pure loving light encircle and envelope you. Pulling you into an ethereal body of joyful, peaceful and loving light. Imagine the warmth and love of God's embrace fully encompass and engulf you.

Surrounding you.

Consuming you.

Imagine God is hugging you.

This is the energy of the angel number 0.

The angel number 0 is a very divine and spiritual number. At first, it may seem as though its energy conflicts with itself and may feel confusing. So, in order to fully understand its energy, we have to look beyond the physical world and beyond our usual conscious understanding. We need to suspend our need for logic and linear thinking.

It is the energy of wholeness and oneness. Everything is one. As such the angel number 0 requires us to let go of the physical world's concept of separateness and see that every individual thing is part of a whole. All a product of one source. A product of one ultimate creator. As God hugs us, we become one.

The angel number 0 has no beginning and no end, yet it is the beginning and it is completion. It is known as the Alpha and the Omega. The start, the finish and everything in between. All equal in importance. It carries the energy of nothing yet brings together and encompasses everything. In the beginning there is nothing and, in the end, there is wholeness.

It is the energy of everything. It is the energy of nothing.

The angel number 0 carries the energy of all the universal energies and what is known as the **God Force**. Which is God's loving light and the energy that pours through everything and connects us all. It represents the energy of our connection and closeness to God and the Universe. It is the creator and the source within each one of us.

The angel number 0 also carries the energy of prayer and meditation.

The closed circle of the angel number 0 has no end, representing infinity and eternity. Also representing potential and choice. Inside the circle is emptiness with plenty of room to fill with whatever you want, yet it is full of whatever you will need.

It also represents the continuous cycles we go through, from the beginning to the end. Each completed cycle contributing to the growth and continuation of the next. Once again, each cycle individual yet connected.

The angel number 0 is also known to represent the beginning of our spiritual journey. At a time when the unknown and uncertainty of what lies ahead is emphasized.

It illustrates going through our spiritual journey on our own, but not alone. This is because you are an individual yet a part of source and therefore a part of everything working for the greater good. You make your own choices and walk your own path, but there are plenty of angels and spiritual guides surrounding you and helping you along the way.

The Message of Angel Number 0

If you have been seeing the angel number 0 repeatedly the message you are receiving from the angels is one of pure divine love. Here is what the angels are telling you.

An Exclamation Point!

The angel number 0 brings the energy of all the

other numbers. It represents infinity and eternity and so its energy is limitless and unending. As such, when it is seen with another number, it is emphasizing and enhancing the message of that number. Just like an exclamation point!

CLOSER TO GOD AND THE UNIVERSE

You are being pulled closer to God and to the Universe. This is a point along your spiritual journey where you are becoming closer to God and the Universe. You are gaining new insight and understanding of your oneness and connectedness with Universal and Source energy. Like the analogy from before, God is hugging you and pulling you into an ethereal body of pure love and light.

NEVER ALONE

When you see the angel number 0 the angels are reminding you that you are always surrounded and part of the spiritual realm. Feeling alone is part of living in the physical realm and part of the journey you are on. But the angels are letting you know this feeling is not accurate. You are a part of and are always surrounded by the angels and God.

A COMPLETION

You may see the angel number 0 when you are the end of or are about to complete something. It may be the end of a relationship, a project or a life phase that you have grown from and are ready to complete and move on from. It can also signal the end of an issue you have been dealing with. Endings and change can be challenging. So the angels want you to know that there are endless cycles of growth you will go through, all with positive aspects you may never even dream of. The angels and God are surrounding you and supporting you as you complete this phase and move on to the next.

The Beginning of a New Journey

Just as the angel number 0 may be a message that you are at the end of a phase, it may also be saying you are at the beginning of a new journey. You may be just starting out on your spiritual journey or you may be at a place where your spiritual journey feels unknown, uncertain and new. Either way, the angels are sending a message to stay positive, have faith and keep going. Although the unknown may seem overwhelming, scary and lonely at times, you are not alone. Once again, the angels and God are surrounding you and supporting you every step of the way.

Look to Your Higher-Self

The angels are sending the message of the angel number 0 to encourage you to seek answers and listen to your higher-self. Pay attention to your intuition as it will guide you toward the answers and understanding you seek.

Look For Signs

By seeing the angel number 0, your message is that God is supporting and comforting you. God is hearing and answering your prayers. Which means now is an important time to actively look for signs, especially after praying or meditating.

Raise Your Vibrations

The angels are encouraging you to raise your vibrations. To receive spiritual help and achieve spiritual growth, you need to have a high energetic vibration. When vibrating at a higher frequency you have a much stronger connection with the spiritual realm. It also makes it easier for the spiritual realm to communicate with you. Therefore, you will be able to communicate with angels, God and your higher-self much easier.

By raising your vibrations, you are lighting your own path. Making it much easier to accomplish your purpose with greater understanding. A high vibrational frequency will attract good and positive things into your life. Manifesting abundance, joy and achieving your dreams.

ANGEL NUMBER 11
"THE DOORWAY"

KEYWORDS:

- ✓ The Spiritual
- ✓ Enlightenment
- ✓ Awakening
- ✓ Mysticism
- ✓ Illumination
- ✓ Intuition
- ✓ Idealism
- ✓ Enthusiasm
- ✓ Vision
- ✓ Creativity
- ✓ Self-expression
- ✓ Sensitivity
- ✓ Beginnings
- ✓ Faith
- ✓ High Vibrations
- ✓ Subconscious
- ✓ Dreams
- ✓ Unrestricted
- ✓ Balance
- ✓ Harmony

THE ENERGY OF ANGEL NUMBER 11

Imagine you are walking down a long hallway. This hallway has a peaceful ethereal energy, not quite like any hallway you have ever been in before. A sense of safety and calmness washes over you. As you slowly continue walking two magnificent doors begin to manifest before you. Upon approaching these doors, you realize the other side contains a world unlike any you've ever known.

It is a world of spirit, intuition, and faith. There is no rhyme or reason to what is there – it just is. You look back and see the world you are coming from is the opposite. It is dense and linear. Containing thought, reasoning, logic and rationality.

If you walk through these doors you will be leaving the reality you know and stepping into a dreamlike world. A world dominated by the subconscious, dreams and mystical wonders – unrestricted by any kind of rational thought.

Walking through these doors is to walk into the energy of the angel number 11.

It is common for the number 11 to be depicted as a doorway. As it carries the energy of spiritual awakening. Our ability to reach spiritual enlightenment. Such as walking through a door and waking up to our spirit, no longer concerned with what the physical world says reality should be.

It is not concerned with any logic or rational thoughts. It is faith. There is no need for reasoning when we lean on faith. As faith is the feeling of knowing… of believing, without explanation.

The angel number 11 is a direct connection to our subconscious and the inner-knowledge and desires that we are not always aware of. It is the most intuitive of all the numbers. With the energy of using feeling, intuition, inspiration and idealism without any rationality.

The angel number 11 also carries the energy of creativity, self-expression and vision. It is the side of ourselves that we allow to dream and see beyond our physical world. It is the energy of illumination, of lighting the way to different, better and more spiritual things.

The energy of psychics, mystics, clairvoyants, prophets, and all those who are not limited by our six senses or confined to the physical world is also a part of the angel number 11's energy.

The angel number 11 has the energy of leading the way and paving new roads. Combined with the energy of faith, balance and harmony.

The angel number 11 is a very intense spiritual energy and its corresponding messages are also intense. If you see this number often you are being called to push yourself to spiritual greatness.

Challenges

When the messages of the angel number 11 are not mastered you may experience its difficult side. Which includes feeling extremely shy, anxious, stressed, conflicted, scattered, and/or fearful. You may also tend to self-sabotage and create needless problems for yourself.

The Message of Angel Number 11

If you repeatedly see the number 11, it is a message from the angels to pay attention and take action. Here is what the angels are telling you.

Check Yourself

Angels will send the angel number 11 to those of us who are unfocused, lack self-confidence and are engaging in self-sabotaging behaviors.

Take a moment to check where your thoughts and behaviors are leading you. Are you on the path of happiness? If not pay attention to the other messages of angel number 11, because it is time for you to make some changes.

Surrounded By Love and Light

No matter where you are in life or along your path, the angels are letting you know that they are surrounding you with love and light.

You are never alone. All you need to do is ask for their assistance and the angels will respond.

A Time of Enlightenment

When the angels show you the angel number 11, it means you can reach spiritual enlightenment. By showing you this number, the angels are illuminating the doorway to change through self-growth and spiritual awakening. The angels are encouraging you to walk through those doors and connect with your higher-self and the spiritual world. Here you will find, understand and know how to accomplish your life's purpose and where your spiritual journey is leading you.

Connect To Your Mission

By seeing the angel number 11 you are receiving a message to find and stay focused on your life purpose. Once again you are being guided to walk through the doors of spiritual awakening. There you can connect with your higher-self and have a clear connection to your soul's mission.

Stay Focused

Once you have an idea of what your mission is, *stay focused* on accomplishing it. Create smaller goals that will help you reach the larger goal(s). The more specific and concrete your goals are the more confident, successful and happy you will be.

If you find that you have been feeling scattered, stressed, anxious, conflicted, shy or experiencing fearful emotions, the angel number 11 is a message that you need to set some solid concrete goals. In addition, it is extremely important for you to maintain your focus on accomplishing them. The angel number 11 is a message that – if you are not staying focused and working toward a goal – you are at high risk of self-sabotage.

Master Positive Thinking

By showing you the angel number 11, the angels are telling you to master positive thinking. Since 11 is a master number, this is more than thinking positive, it is an urgent message for you to MASTER *the art of positive thinking.*

You are manifesting what you think about almost instantly. Your thoughts, positive affirmations and overall optimism will manifest your desires. They will also assist you with accomplishing your goals and understanding your life-purpose. So the angel number 11 is often a warning to stay positive and not to let your positive thinking guard down.

Release Negativity and Fear

In addition to learning to master positive thinking,

the angels are telling you to release all negativity and fear. It is time for you to have a fresh start that includes letting go of the past and staying focused on your desires, goals and purpose. Fear and negativity serve no purpose other than feed your ego, hold you back and encourage self-sabotaging behaviors. Release the past and go forward in faith.

Rationalizing Too Much

The angel number 11 is the number of faith. The angels are letting you know you need to learn to rely on faith rather than logic.

You are at a point in this lifetime where to truly accomplish your soul's mission, you need to let go of control and let the pieces fall. Have faith and believe that who you are, what you have done and your connection to the spiritual realm will ensure the pieces fall exactly where they are meant to. Use your intuition and feelings to connect with your subconscious and higher-self. Let faith be your guiding light.

You Have a Duty to Others

You are meant to be a spiritual leader. To guide and illuminate the way for others on their spiritual journey and as they walk their life path. The angel number 11 is a calling for you to recognize your importance as a light-worker and to guide and inspire others.

ANGEL NUMBER 22
"DREAM MAKER"

KEYWORDS:

- ✓ Ambition
- ✓ Accomplishment
- ✓ Manifestation
- ✓ Making the impossible possible
- ✓ Power
- ✓ Reality
- ✓ Builders
- ✓ Masters
- ✓ Idealistic
- ✓ Possibilities
- ✓ Potential
- ✓ Perseverance
- ✓ Determination
- ✓ Expansion
- ✓ Insight
- ✓ Desires
- ✓ The greater good
- ✓ Philanthropy
- ✓ Dreaming
- ✓ Believing
- ✓ Creating
- ✓ Life Purpose
- ✓ The Soul's Mission

THE ENERGY OF ANGEL NUMBER 22

The angel number 22 is the representation of our ability to make dreams come true. It is the energy of accomplishment and manifestation. But it isn't the accomplishment of just any ordinary dream or goal. It is the power and accomplishment to bring into reality what *seems* impossible.

The angel number 22 expands on the high ideals and unrestricted imagination of the angel number 11 and uses the earthly energies of the angel number 4 to turn them into reality.

The angel number 22 is like having your head in the clouds and your feet on the ground at the same time. It is having faith, believing and imagining without rationality and using pragmatism, organization and rationality to make it happen.

It is reaching for the stars and bringing them down to earth. With the energy of the angel number 22, you can make the impossible possible.

Known as the most powerful of all the numbers, the angel number 22 carries the energy of commanding manifestation. Manifestation so strong that nothing can stop what we want from coming into reality.

In fact, those who are born with a life path number of 22 are known as the Master Builders. They are the people who can dream up great idealistic things and use determination, devotion, self-control and good organization and management skills to build them.

The angel number 22 carries the energy of not giving up on anything. Even when things are not working out as you expect, the energy of the angel number 22 encourages you to keep going. Either believing the hard work will pay off or something different than expected will come from your efforts. This is how great empires are built. With the energy of persistence, determination and ambition inherent in the angel number 22.

This extreme power of the angel number 22 is all

about the divine life purpose and the soul's mission. No matter what your dreams are, if it pertains to your soul's mission nothing will stop it from happening. People who see the angel number 22 have a great deal to accomplish. They are meant to build something greater than themselves to make the world a better place.

It is the energy of manifesting, ambition, idealism and desires. It resonates with the energies of personal power, intuition, adaptability, expansion, insight, and sensitivity combined with pragmaticism, confidence, discipline and balance. Such a powerful combination of energies can turn any goal or dream into a reality.

It is the energy of dreaming, believing and having faith along with creating strong foundations, being grounded, and having stability and security. As such the angel number 22 is the energy of power and accomplishment. It is dreaming without restraint, believing in the possibilities and creating with determination.

It also carries the energy of philanthropy and service to others. Much of the powerful energy of angel number 22 is about compassion and the soul's mission to serve the greater good. Expanding and evolving the physical plane into a safer and more abundant place for everyone.

Challenges

When the messages of the angel number 22 are not mastered you may experience its difficult side. Which includes being unorganized, careless, overwhelmed, unable to focus, nervous, impractical and suffering from excessive self-imposed pressure. To not listen to the messages of the angel number 22 you may miss out on opportunities and shy away from potential possibilities of greatness.

THE MESSAGE OF ANGEL NUMBER 22

If you repeatedly see the number 22, it is a message from the angels to make your dreams come true. Here is what the angels are telling you.

YOU ARE MORE

Often the angels will show you the angel number 22 when you are not living up to your potential. This may be because you are not aware of your own capabilities or it may be because you are living with doubt about what you are truly capable of.

By seeing the angel number 22 the angels are letting you know that you have the power and ability to make your dreams and goals come true no matter how out of reach they may seem to you right now.

The angels are showing you that your life purpose is important. You are meant to build something that will make a difference. Pay attention to the messages of the angel number 22 to help you achieve and accomplish all that you are meant to be.

BUILD YOUR DREAMS

At this time, the angels are calling on you to find your passion. Dream up big things and create high lofty goals related to what you are passionate about. The dreams, goals and passion you have are related to your life purpose and soul's mission, and, as such, are fully supported by the angels.

The angels are cautioning you to not shy away from your passion and dreams. You are now meant to dream big and challenge yourself to accomplish it all. No dream is too ambitious with the power of the angel number 22 on your side.

Believe In Yourself

When sending the message of the angel number 22, the angels are encouraging you to let go of doubts about yourself and your ability to accomplish your goals. They are letting you know that you have what it takes to accomplish great things. Have faith in yourself and your abilities.

Free Yourself

When you see the angel number 22, you are being guided to free yourself from any binds or blocks that are holding you back. This includes breaking free from your past and from the confines of your comfort zone.

It is important for you to heal from your past so you can let go of what no longer serves you. Often, we hold on to past experiences and traumas that keep us from moving on and growing spiritually. The angels are encouraging you to take an inventory of past experiences and free yourself from any holds it has on you.

Your comfort zone may also be holding you back. Your comfort zone will only serve to keep you where you are and does not allow for growth. Now is the time to take some risks, challenge yourself and act on your dreams and desires.

Listen to your intuition and act accordingly. The angels are surrounding you and letting you know it is safe to take chances.

You will be amazed at what you can accomplish by letting go and freeing yourself from these binds.

Create Balance and Harmony

The angels are encouraging you to create balance and harmony in all aspects of your life. Be sure to balance work with self-care, giving with receiving and pay attention to the relationships in your life. Including the relationship you have with yourself.

Look at all aspects in your life and be sure nothing is one-sided. The message of the angel number 22 stresses a great need to master having this balance in all areas of your life.

Be Practical

The angel number 22 is a message to be practical and pragmatic when working towards your goals. You are being guided to dream big without restraint, but it is by being practical and pragmatic that you will be able to make those dreams a reality. Do not let your emotions rule this situation, it is a time for logic and rationality.

If you are feeling overwhelmed, nervous, unorganized, unable to focus and have a fear of taking risks, make sure you are grounded and have a practical focus on how you are going about things. See the angel number 4 to assist you more with this. By doing so you will feel more in control and capable of accomplishing just about anything and fulfilling your life purpose.

You Are a Powerful Manifestor

When you see the angel number 22, the angels are telling you that you are a very powerful manifestor right now. What you are thinking about, dreaming about and planning are all coming to fruition very quickly. Be sure to stay focused on what you really want and once again dream big because you are in the ideal place to make the impossible possible.

Focus On Your Life Path

By seeing the angel number 22 the angels are encouraging you to find and focus on your life purpose. You are meant to build something bigger than yourself and to make a difference in the world. Your life purpose includes being a leader and being of service to others. So, if you have been considering going into business for yourself or creating something big now is the time to do it.

Work diligently with integrity and devotion to build something great, accomplish your dreams and follow your soul's mission. The angels are letting you know that by using your inner-wisdom, having faith and believing in yourself you will succeed. In fact, the hard work you have already put in is paying off. So, keep going.

Angel Number 33
"Pass It On"

Keywords:

- ✓ Love
- ✓ Compassion
- ✓ Blessings
- ✓ Emotions
- ✓ Influence
- ✓ Inspiration
- ✓ Courage
- ✓ Honesty
- ✓ Factual
- ✓ Guidance
- ✓ Teaching
- ✓ Healing
- ✓ Helping
- ✓ Idealistic
- ✓ Responsible
- ✓ Supportive
- ✓ Uplifting
- ✓ Devoted
- ✓ Sensible
- ✓ Selflessness
- ✓ Giving
- ✓ Sincerity
- ✓ Family Oriented
- ✓ Loving Discipline
- ✓ Self-expression
- ✓ Spirituality
- ✓ Ascended Masters

The Energy of Angel Number 33

The angel number 33 is a very spiritual and emotional number. It carries the energy of many spiritual and religious aspects. Such as the ascended masters, the holy trinity and the third eye. It is the energy of our physical lives being connected and intertwined with the spiritual.

Seeing this number after prayer, meditation or using positive affirmations means your prayers have been heard and are being answered.

The angel number 33 resonates with a very high, positive, nurturing and uplifting energy.

It is the embodiment of love and caring and the desire to teach and help others. Because of this energy, it is known as the most influential of all the numbers.

To fully grasp the energy of the angel number 33 you can look to the ascended masters. Those who teach us that all things are possible especially when you act with love and for the greater good. The angel number 33 is the number of ascended masters. And therefore, embodies the influential nature and spiritual mastery of these leaders.

The ascended masters view the world and all its inhabitants with unconditional positive regard. They are influential teachers of love. Healers and selfless helpers of all people. They reach out and uplift the physical world to heightened levels of spiritual enlightenment.

The angel number 33 carries joy, optimism creativity and the youthful energies of the angel number 3 double and combines it with the nurturing energies of the angel number 6. It is the energy of blessings, compassion, helping, guidance and inspiration. It also resonates with the energy of courage, loving discipline and honesty.

The angel number 33 builds upon the spiritual purity of the master number 11 and the ability to make the impossible possible of the master number 22. Combining and building upon these energies the angel number 33 passes these powerful energies on to others as loving, thoughtful and factual spiritual guidance.

The energy of the angel number 33 teaches us to love ourselves and others equally. It encourages us to reach out and touch the lives of others. Teaching them, healing them and loving them.

It is the energy of selfless service done with joy, love and optimism. It is the energy of the teachers of truth, love and compassion. Those who have an innately powerful ability to influence others.

The energy of the angel number 33 is idealistic, supportive, devoted and sincere. It is joyful and selfless.

The angel number 33 has a very loving, spiritual and influential energy. Those who frequently see the angel number 33 are guided to selflessly learn and pass on spiritual guidance, help and healing. They are encouraged to find ways to creatively teach others what they learn. To uplift and empower the world around them.

CHALLENGES

When the messages of the angel number 33 are not mastered you may experience its difficult side. Which includes being a perfectionist and overbearing on yourself and others, critical, meddling, irresponsible, indulgent, self-absorbed, self-destructive, easily disappointed and crippled with strong negative emotions. The challenges of the angel number 33 may also lead to addictions and other self-defeating coping skills.

THE MESSAGE OF ANGEL NUMBER 33

If you repeatedly see the number 33, it is a message from the angels to love yourself and pass it on. Here is what the angels are telling you.

YOU'RE HOLDING YOURSELF BACK

The angel number 33 is commonly seen by those feeling overwhelmed and incapable of achieving their goals and dreams even though they are on the right path and are living a spiritual life. In other words, you're doing everything right, but your thoughts and emotions are getting in the way.

The angels are encouraging you to find your own inner-peace and trust in yourself, your talents and your instincts.

This is a message of your being capable and already doing things right, but your need for perfectionism and control is holding you back from your purpose. You may even appear to be critical and judgmental of yourself or others due to your need to get everything exactly right. This need for perfection is holding you back from achieving your purpose.

The angels want you to know that you are important and have what it takes to accomplish your goals and live according to your purpose. Trust your instincts and pay attention to the messages of the angel number 33 to help you overcome any obstacles holding you back.

You Have A Spiritual Purpose

By seeing the angel number 33, the angels are saying you have a spiritual life purpose. They are encouraging you to focus on your spiritual nature and abilities. You are meant to heal, inspire, teach, create and bring love into the world. The ability to do so will come naturally for you.

Focus on bringing more love into the world and to the world's inhabitants. Use your natural creative ability to reach people in new ways and to help and heal. The joy you receive from giving and helping is infectious and will influence the world and the people around you in very positive ways.

An Ascended Master is With You

When you see the angel number 33 the angels are showing you that your connection to an ascended master is strong. This ascended master is supporting, guiding, assisting and protecting you.

Ascended masters help us to manifest desires, find peace, understanding and love, and they help us see ourselves and others through the eyes of God.

Your assistance may be coming from any of the ascended masters you feel a strong connection with. Including Jesus, Buddha, Quan Yin, a saint or any spiritual or religious figure.

This is a sign to let go of fear and doubt and walk in faith. You will receive assistance for whatever projects or changes you are considering. So, you are being encouraged to go through with them. There is no need for worry or concern. You are being protected and taken care of.

Work on Inner-Balance

The angel number 33 is a message to work on having strong inner-balance. You may be in a place where you are experiencing some very strong emotions. Including extremes of both positive and negative emotions. These emotions can feel overwhelming and get the best of you.

To deal with these emotions, the angels are encouraging you to focus on your spiritual connection and create balance within. Do this by confronting your own "stuff." Look inward and heal yourself. Let go of what no longer serves you and realize that your past does not define your life or who you are.

This is a call to find your true-self and understand who you really are amongst all the chaos of living a physical life in a physical world. Seek balance between your current physical existence and your spiritual connection.

Priorities are Paramount

The angel number 33 is a call to find and focus on your priorities. Those who frequently see the angel number 33 tend to take on too much and try to be everything to everyone all the time. The angels are encouraging you to learn to say "no" and keep your focus on what is most important to you.

Don't spread yourself too thin. Figure out what

your priorities are and put your focus on them.

SEE THE WHOLE SITUATION

If you are currently facing a difficult situation or a problem, the angel number 33 is letting you know to look at the situation as a whole picture. Avoid getting caught up in the details.

Take a step back and remove yourself from the situation so you can clearly see it for what it is. Be sure to double check the facts, as the angel number 33 carries the energy of well-informed and researched information.

HELP, BUT DON'T CONTROL

The message of the angel number 33 encourages you to focus on spreading love and helping others. However, it is also a message to let go of the need to help everyone.

There are those who are just not willing to accept your help and you need to be able to accept that and let it go. To continue trying to help them becomes meddling and controlling and will push people away and discourage them.

Allow others to take responsibility for their own actions. Treat them with love and offer help but understand not everyone will accept it. The angels are reminding you to take care to not feel disappointed when others are unwilling to change or accept your help.

Keep in mind, we all must walk our own path and have our own journey to take. Not everyone will see the world the way you do. Everything happens for a reason and sometimes we need to let people go their own way – even if you know they may wind up worse off. Let those people go and instead focus on helping those who want it.

Love Yourself – Then Help

The angel number 33 is a call from the angels to MASTER loving yourself and knowing yourself before you help others. Really get to know yourself and who you are. What are your goals, desires, ideals? What is most important to *you* and what is the best way for *you* to achieve it?

Once you really understand yourself, your talents, and your instincts embrace and use them to assist and heal others. The angels are letting you know that it is very important for you to work on yourself and have a deep loving relationship with yourself before you can serve your purpose of spreading love and helping and healing others.

CONCLUSION

I'd like to end this book by saying thank you. First, I want to thank my children who have supported and helped me with this book every step of the way. They are the inspiration and the motivation that keeps me going each and every day. I also want to thank the angels who have given me the gift of writing and gave me the words to put on each page. Last, but certainly not least, I want to thank you, the reader. You are the reason and the purpose for writing this book. I am so very grateful for every one of you. It is my hope that through this book you have found a path that brings you closer to the love and light the angels bring into our physical existence.

When I first began writing this book I thought it would be a short guide. Yet as I began writing and asking the angels to provide me with the information they wanted you (the reader) to know, more and more information came to me. Resulting in a much longer book than I anticipated. This just goes to show how much the world of angel numbers has to offer us. They range from being simple signs and messages from the angels letting us know they are with us, guiding us and loving us to being an in-depth and complex form of communication. The amazing thing is, the choice is yours. Angels, angel numbers, and any kind of angel communication adapts and molds into the perfect fit for anyone. Whatever fits best into your life and your needs will work and will result in miracles. Writing this book has truly been an amazing experience for me that I will cherish for many years to come.

I urge you to take what you have learned a step further. Make angel numbers your own personal experience with the angels. Your relationship with the angels is unique and personal. Develop your use of angel number messages so that they reflect that relationship in your life. Angel numbers helped change the way I feel about and experience my life by helping end my depression and guiding me through each day. I used to feel lost and alone in the world, now I feel surrounded and loved by an eternal family that transcends the physical world. What will angel numbers do for you? Don't be limited by my experience or my words and ideas, let your experience with angel numbers bloom and blossom into an exceptional and amazing experience of your own.

Although I chose to title this book *Angel Numbers Mastery,* I am certain there is a whole world of angel numbers, and what they mean for us, still to be explored and discovered. As our planet and the people on it evolve and awaken in their spirituality, angel numbers and the way we connect with angels may grow into something awesome and currently unimaginable. Where peace, love and blessings becoming the norm for all. I have no doubt it is by learning and connecting with each other in love and support we will bring about a planetary awakening that involves the spiritual becoming part of everyone's experience. Changing life as we know it. It all starts with us. Our open hearts, our open minds and passing on what we have learned with love to others. So, keep learning, exploring and channeling the angels and their energy. Each step you take brings the vibrational energy of our planet closer to something truly amazing.

With love and blessings,

Sarahdawn

ABOUT THE AUTHOR

Sarahdawn Tunis holds a B.A. in counseling psychology from Fort Lewis College and M.A. in Counseling Psychology and Counselor Education with an emphasis in Couples and Families from the University of Colorado at Denver. Sarahdawn worked for several years in private practice specializing in mood disorders, couples counseling and counseling families with special needs children. Eventually, Sarahdawn's calling led her to the metaphysical and spiritual aspects of healing and growth. As witness to the power of spirit for easing the pain and struggles of this physical life, Sarahdawn is now dedicated to helping others discover their own path and personal power through the angels, spirituality and the metaphysical aspects of our life on earth.

You can learn more about Sarahdawn and her works at SarahdawnTunis.com.

Source Notes

Center for Disease Control. *One in Three Adults Don't Get Enough Sleep.*
https://www.cdc.gov/media/releases/2016/p0215-enough-sleep.html

Decoz, Hans. *Master Numbers.*
https://www.worldnumerology.com/numerology-master-numbers.htm

Numerology.com. *Get Free Numerology Report and Decode the Patterns of the Universe.*
https://www.numerology.com/

Shakespeare, William (1989). The Unabridged William Shakespeare. *Hamlet* 1.5.167—8. Philadelphia, PA, The Running Press.

Tunis, Sarahdawn. *An Easy Guide to Angel Numbers.*
https://www.sarahdawntunis.com/angel-numbers

Virtue, Doreen. (2007). *How to Hear Your Angels.* Carlsbad, CA, Hay House, Inc.

Virtue, Doreen. (2008). *Angel Numbers 101.* Carlsbad, CA, Hay House, Inc.

Walmsley, Joanne. *Angel Numbers.* Joanne Sacred Scribes.
http://sacredscribesangelnumbers.blogspot.com/p/vibrations-of-numbers-0-to-10.html

Sarahdawn Tunis
Dreaming, Believing, Becoming

www.SarahdawnTunis.com
If you found this book helpful please consider leaving a review.
Your feedback, comments and suggestions are welcome. Send messages to:
sarah@sarahdawntunis.com.
Mail correspondence to P.O. Box 150846 Lakewood, CO 80215

Thank you for reading! Love, light & blessings. <3

Printed in Great Britain
by Amazon